CONQUISTADOR

By Philip Guedalla

PALMERSTON

FATHERS OF THE REVOLUTION

THE SECOND EMPIRE

A GALLERY

MASTERS AND MEN

SUPERS AND SUPERMEN

CONQUISTADOR

AMERICAN FANTASIA

by

Philip Guedalla

Ah! me arm aches, and the sleeve of me little coat is wore; I am so eager to write it all off to me ant.

GEORGE MOORE

What with the railroads a-fuzzing and a-whizzing, I'm clean stonied, muddled and beat.

FITZJAMES STEPHEN

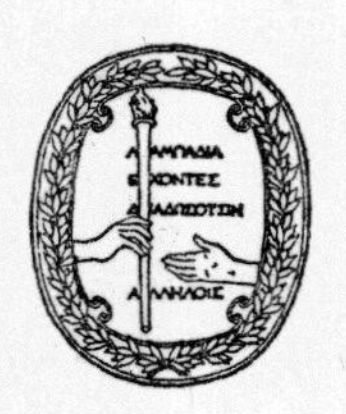

NEW YORK AND LONDON

Harper & Brothers Publishers

1 9 2 8

CONQUISTADOR

PRINTED IN THE U.S.A.

D-C

To
My Charming Guardians
The Pullman Porters of America

PASSPORT

". . . to pass freely without let or hindrance, and to afford him every assistance and protection of which he may stand in need." *The urbane request concluded in a smother of armorial bearings, and the voice fell silent. It seemed to come from very far away. For it was the voice (so the inscription ran) of George Nathaniel, Marquess Curzon of Kedleston, Earl of Kedleston, Viscount Scarsdale, Baron Ravensdale, Knight of the Most Noble Order of the Garter, a Member of His Britannic Majesty's Most Honourable Privy Council, Knight Grand Commander of the Most Exalted Order of the Star of India, Knight Grand Commander of the Most Eminent Order of the Indian Empire, etc., etc., etc., His Majesty's Principal Secretary of State for Foreign Affairs. From beyond the clouds, seated sedately in the most exclusive company of all, that stately form seemed to direct my Odyssey, as other Olympians my predecessor's after another war. Surely Zeus himself was my protector; and as he waved me on, perhaps the broad shoulders (frock-coated even in the Hereafter) shook with invisible amusement. For under that august protection one more child of the Old World was setting out to try conclusions with the New—another Daniel come to judgment, and a little nervous of the lions.*

The approach was simple and romantic. How few of us

confess the rich romance with which Englishmen regard the United States. The lure is not in their wide horizons (for we have wide horizons of our own), nor in those bright financial prospects which Anglo-Saxons have agreed to term 'opportunity.' Let others feel that spell. Latins, sunk in their Mediterranean slumbers, may yield themselves to the illusion that new countries throb with romance. But Englishmen, whose dismal fate it is to settle them, know that new countries are the least romantic. Why, otherwise, the annual pilgrimage of a New World in systematic search of romance in the Old? Besides, what places in the modern world are really newer than their fellows? Are they not all, since the Industrial Revolution, of the same age—the age of their machinery? Two cities in two hemispheres, each devoted with a common gesture to the production of cheap automobiles, are filled with corresponding plants and consecrated to the same unpretending mission. Which is the elder? For in each identical machinery was installed at the same moment. Surely Detroit and Coventry are sisters, however flattering it may appear to regard the one as a stupendous child, the other as a gallant parent. For newness is not a quality confined to the New World. It was new once, of course, when the first caravels voyaged uncertainly towards it and landing-parties asked startled Mohawks to direct them to the Great Cham of Tartary. It was still new, when rifles cracked in the great woods and lonely birds wheeled watchfully round the infrequent smoke of cabins. But in those years the Old World was growing new as well. A Frontier called (and pioneers responded), when half England moved northwards in pursuit of coal and made its clearings in the woods, its settlements among the Yorkshire moors and on the bare hillsides of Lancashire. For we all have our Covered Waggons.

The American appeal owes little to its newness. It grows, for Englishmen, on the far richer soil of genuine romance. Somewhere beyond the sunset dwells, to our heated fancy, a fairyland of incredible things—of Oberons incalculably rich, of Titanias lovely beyond the dreams of younger sons, of lesser fairies lit with the fairy glow of Kleig lights and dancing in their rings where the sea meets the Beverly Hills below Hollywood. That Elfland's horns may sometimes be encountered not too faintly calling in our dance-music, its fairies on our screens; its Puck, the bootlegger, performs his miracles whenever we go to the theatre; and as we open any magazine, its magic is all about us. For, to the British mind, America is now the land of dreams-come-true. Our fathers knew it only as the home of redskins, buffaloes, and Colt revolvers, peopled by scouts, confidence-men, and slightly sententious darkies. But, for us, that air is heavy with high-jacking, automatics, Romneys, corners in wheat, First Folios, and all the rich scents of modern piracy. The whole continent is one big Treasure Island, with blind Pew tapping at every corner and a hope (how rarely realised) of Long John Silver at the White House. Small wonder that we thrill at thoughts of the land where everything is possible—the late William Jennings Bryan, syncopation, Henry Ford, Niagara, Miss Gertrude Stein, Prohibition, Mr. Sinclair Lewis, earth-

quake, flood, William Hale Thompson, and all the latest wonders of the world.

Here is romance for jaded palates, and we throb responsive. Not otherwise intrepid maiden ladies of uncertain age glowed with romance, as the steam-packet bore them from the trim lawns of Lord Palmerston's England, past the bright railings of the Second Empire, to the heaped skylines of romantic Sicily. For in Sicily anything might happen—banditti *in delicious pointed hats, cross-gartered muleteers, a handsome goatherd, ransoms and rescues, and the delicate attentions of Her Majesty's Vice-Consul at Catania.*

Romance, which came (like nearly everything) out of the East, follows the sun; and as we strain our eyes across the sea we catch the glow of its stupendous setting in the West. For it was eastern, when we first learned to be romantic. The earliest figures of romance came, riding attenuated chargers, out of the desert; and for a while their scimitar, their burnous, and their dark Zuleika engaged us. Then the focus of romance shifted a little westward, and the heroic Greek replaced the Bedouin. The vogue was all for Klephts and yataghans and Palikars and broken columns. Westward again (to be precise, a little north of west), until for a brief, incredible interlude Germany became the home of romance; and ragged clouds drifted with hooting owls above ruined castles on the Rhine. Still westward, till the castanets sounded the authentic note of romance a few years later, as Carmencita and her contrabandistas *strode gallantly into the hard Andalusian sunlight and took their rakish poses. But in Spain the moving finger of romance had touched the edge of Europe. Quite unperturbed, it crossed the Atlantic.*

That, perhaps, is how America became to British eyes the last citadel of romance, outlined against the West with its small, gesticulating figures etched sharply on the glow behind them. What Childe Roland worthy of his spurs would not ride out to such a Dark Tower and sound his horn?

The approach, I think I wrote, was quite romantic. And the return? Knights errant are often highly reticent after the quest is over. An exhausted charger ambles up the hill; the castle gates clang to behind it; and we are left outside, in doubt as to the temper of the dragon and even the beauty of the maid. Was there, we sometimes wonder, a maid at all? So, also, the intrepid female, homeward bound from Sicily, creeps all unravished back to Cheltenham. And, wiser (perhaps) than I, both knight and lady keep their own counsel. Yet I feel that silence would be unmannerly. Besides, it is so tempting for a traveller to tell traveller's tales.

These, then, are a few traveller's tales. Before I tell them, let me explain their limitations. Three months, which is a long time for any traveller, is a short time for the United States; and though the road from Central Park to the Rio Grande, out to the Golden Gate and back again is long as well, it is not long enough for any man to learn a continent. Perhaps he may unlearn; but there was little time for learning. So there is no attempt here at any ordered survey of the past, present, and immediate prospects of the United States (with maps, appendices, and a posthumous Introduction by Lord Bryce). The object of these pages is far humbler. Having crawled, buzzing slightly, across a vast window-pane, I felt that news of my adventure might interest some of the other flies—and, perhaps, the pane itself. I have described a surface; and surfaces, I warn the student, are superficial. Deeper studies may be safely left to those whose stay was briefer still.

So I compile my traveller's tales. The journey, as I have hinted, was wildly exciting. How far the excitement held, where it collapsed and when it rose again, the tales themselves may show. But they cannot render the continuous surprise that any visitor must feel as a large continent gives him a gracious welcome. So that grateful astonishment of his must be the undertone of accompaniment to all these tales, the drone of my little bagpipes. For my thanks are all omitted. No private names stand in these pages, either for good or evil. My hostesses and hosts (and how clearly I see them, on docks and railway platforms, platforms of public halls, and in those dreadful little rooms behind the platform where hurried speakers meet their chairmen; seated in kindly rows, or standing in alarming circles; but always welcoming—at doors, in hotel lobbies, halls, and dining-rooms—hospitably wielding tea-pots, coffee-pots, and utensils even less hallowed by the law), my hosts and hostesses, alas! are all unnamed. So is the citizen who borrowed my umbrella on the train between Minneapolis and Cedar Rapids, Ia. For it seemed fairer so.

I present my passport, then. One pair of eyes, item *of*

ears, both reinforced by a consuming interest in nearly everything, must constitute my only claim to enter. And now may I begin my traveller's tales? I have heard better ones. But they were someone else's—and that would be cheating.

PHILIP GUEDALLA.

1927.

CONTENTS

SEA-PIECE

SEA-PIECE
(*mid-winter*)

LIT, like the House of Commons, from above (but with better music), the big brown room swung gently on the North Atlantic. The shaded lights hinted discreetly at the *décor* of some indeterminate Louis; and, Louis no less, chairs of remotely Gallic ancestry stood round the little tables with a silent hint of conviviality. Less mute in its appeal, but equally convivial, the band played on behind its undergrowth on the big dais at the end. It played *Aïda* with tremendous emphasis (that march, with its terrific opening for horns that opens upon nothing, always recalls the vast portico in front of Euston Station); it wrung our hearts with the last, strident moments of unhappy *Butterfly;* and sometimes (but this was in the evenings) it wailed the very latest invitation to the dance with a gently thudding drum and saxophones hooting low. It ran up and down the whole rich gamut of restaurant music before our inattentive ears as we sat, drooping a little, in the *décor* of whatever Louis to hear the music of whatever *maestro*.

For we were undeniably dispirited. The lights, the band, the little tables, and the whole illusion of a vast hotel were spread before our unappreciative eyes, and we stared at them in ungrateful apathy. How wonderful it was to sit there beyond Land's End, ordering drinks and listening to the music. We told ourselves how wonderful it was at frequent intervals. But nothing responded; no spark within our listening hearts leapt up to greet the miracle, as we sat drooping in our chairs. Not ours the fierce, almost professional enjoyment of any problem in wholesale catering successfully overcome that lights Mr. Arnold Bennett on his way through the hotel lounges of the world. How eagerly he would have counted all the forks, fingered how lovingly each delicious tap in our secluded bathrooms. For him the romance of large hotels has surely effaced the mystery of the sea, promoting Ritz and Statler over the heads of Drake and Nelson. Yet Drakes, in a sense, ourselves, we sat at small round tables in mid-ocean; and as the fox-trot moaned, the ferns in front of it quivered a little to the throbbing engines, and the big brown room swung gently on the North Atlantic.

Outside, dark mountains veined like marble, stretched endlessly away to a low sky-line. It was a tumbled country of flung hills and valleys, of sharply tilted slopes and valley-floors that rose suddenly to be crest-lines in a lunar landscape of tormented mountains, all coloured to a noble hue and veined like marble; and it ran quite unbrokenly from our cut-water to the low sky-line, where America waited somewhere behind the mists. It was a silent county, except where it ran hissing past the port-holes; and as we toiled across it at unusual angles, it seemed to watch from all its summits a little sullenly, staring without a sound. Sometimes a plume of smoke stained its horizon at the distant rim, or another traveller was seen for an instant labouring up a long acclivity; and once an ostrich-feather, drooping and white, appeared upon its surface, propelled by a black rectangle that vaguely recalled a four-wheeled cab and indicated (to less terrene eyes) a whale. Someone, forgetting the hotel behind us, said, "There she blows"; inmates of literary tendencies remembered *Moby Dick,* whilst eager neighbours asked hopefully for icebergs, and for an instant we almost seemed to be at sea. But the long journey was resumed across the endless upland, where the blue hills stood in long ranges, and we went smoothly past their marble slopes without a sound.

There was a sound, though. Inaudible on deck, sea-fanciers will recall it as the authentic music of the sea. For the inner parts of ships (and, after all, it was a ship) are filled with an unceasing creak. The little rooms, that look so decorous and still, creak suddenly behind their Adam mirrors as if to startle unwary inmates with a sudden intimation of the sea. The trim joinery of their panels and the neat mouldings, all so impeccably terrestrial, seem to deny the imputation. But the creak belies them. Speaking suddenly, and low, it betrays the sea behind the walls; and, obedient to their real master, the little rooms stand creaking all night long, the bathrooms creak among their perfect plumbing, and the long passages are bronchial with creaking. Even the big brown room upstairs, lit (like the House of Commons) from above, creaks gently from behind its panels of whatever Louis; and when the saxophones drop to a confidential note, one can hear the sea above them talking in its unpleasant whisper.

LANDFALL

LANDFALL

STRANGELY unobtrusive, America steals upon the explorer—not otherwise, perhaps, than a light ahead gleamed through the autumn dusk of an October night in 1492 to a small sailing-ship named *Santa Maria*, and the captain began to throw the drinks overboard. For he knew that he had discovered America. One can almost see the scene—the sad faces of the Spanish sailors in the waist of the little ship, the waiting barrels on the deck, Columbus' muttered words of a farewell to a favourite hogshead, and then a dismal splash. . . .

That is, no doubt, the version of Columbus' landfall that will be taught in the schools of the Republic, when the facts have been brought into a becoming conformity with the Eighteenth Amendment. And why not? Was not a grotesque election once fought by an extremely able man in the second city of the Union upon the simple but alluring issue of amending its school text-books into line with some of his supporters' prejudices? For that judicious statesman demanded ampler recognition for the Revolutionary services of Washington's Irish (Irish abounded in his constituency), as well as of his Germans (Chicago was once termed the sixth German city in the world) and his

Poles (nor were Polish names unknown upon the voters' lists); indeed, irreverent conjecture hinted that, being already sure of the Negro vote, he made no historical claim for Washington's Negroes.

As any student of democracy could have foretold, he won the election. He won it mainly by a free use of the compelling cry "America First." And, again, why not? What country could resist that appeal? Not mine, I think; nor France (for even the sluggish blood of Europe can be made to pulse more quickly with the raw wine of patriotism); but, least of all, his own, devoted by a long and glorious tradition to all the exercises of organised emotion heightened by the very last devices of publicity—the nobly waving flag, the soundly beaten drum, the rich eloquence of Conventions, and annual holocausts of Fourth of July firecrackers. So one had half expected some stupendous intimation of all the wonders that lay in waiting a mile or so ahead—a fanfare of headlines, flourish of posters, tucket of sky-signs, or a grand set-piece of advertisement with linguistic rockets starred along the zenith and Catherine-wheels of appreciation revolving in mute ecstasy.

But the landfall was oddly unobtrusive. For America steals on the explorer out of the morning mist. The big blue mountains of mid-ocean were far behind us now; and smooth levels of grey water sliding past presently disclosed an indubitably American tanker, followed by real American gulls and by mud-flats yet more real. Then (o Columbus; o Amerigo Vespucci) islets took shape and slid away into the mist. A dreary coast-line heaved slowly into the morning; and even the sharp angles of coast-defences failed to lend dignity to Staten Island. For there is little of Gibraltar about Fort Wadsworth. The coast itself seems slightly incredulous; and that rectangular silhouette, which guards the approaches of strong places and awes visitors to Mertz with a sense of guns invisibly in waiting behind the shaven green of smooth escarpments, seems somehow out of place in full view of Coney Island. For one had not looked for guns of position among the switchbacks. Then, our engines running easily for the first time in six days, the Narrows slid past; Liberty, avoiding the obvious by a praiseworthy effort, was small beyond expectation, a greenish miniature of her enormous fame; and the ecstatic watchers on the deck saw tall, unlikely towers step suddenly out of the mist and group themselves into a city.

But down below, where the baggage waited neatly stacked outside relinquished state-rooms, the anxious voices still enquired along each sounding passage for the Something Sisters and the Marchese della Cosa, as an eager Press reached out its tentacles to embrace those paragons of dance and diplomacy, the pride of our ship's company. Perhaps it found them, though I never saw the photographic record of their smiles, the full statement of their feelings on the sky-line, thoughts on war-debts, play censorship, the current trial and the latest book, which are the toll exacted by the enquiring gate-keepers of the New World. One envies Christopher Columbus, to whom the sky-line, at any rate, must have presented a simpler problem when he met the Sioux reporters. For in the somewhat uneventful landscape of Ambrose Channel the wary Genoese might well reply that he had not noticed one. But that excuse now lies far beyond the reach of the least observant mariner. So we admired it, each after his own fashion and to his appropriate reporter—the Something Sisters in duet, the Marchese with a touch of Latin fire, myself with a nervous gesture of propitiation. We admired the United States as well. True, we had not yet set foot in them. But if the ancients could sacrifice to an Unknown God, why not a cautious modern?

So the unlikely towers climbed slowly up the sky; ferry-boats scuttled away to safety; and the Hudson discharged discoloured ice-floes in untidy welcome of the arriving mariners, as the advancing city engulfed us—Marchese, Sisters, smoke-stacks, masts, and all. Tugs, with the consequential air inseparable from tugs in every port, took charge. A deft turn, and we were neatly anchored in a back street, where big black locomotives, hooting huskily, clanged the authentic bells of romance and propelled the right, the real, the inimitable cow-catcher. The New World called, and a scared explorer walked quickly down a gang-plank into it.

VILLE LUMIÈRE

VILLE LUMIÈRE

THE arrival was fantastic—a crowd of tiny sky-scrapers clustering at the water's edge to watch the big ship coming up the Bay; a slow dance of buildings, edging in front of one another to see us rounding the Battery; and then, at some invisible wave of the wand, a piled city standing quite motionless. Etched on the winter sky, it seemed to wait, struck into immobility and bearing its buildings up like some enormous Caryatid. The monstrous silhouette stood waiting; and as the massed buildings stared across the water, one saw for the first time architecture quite unadulterated, *sans* background, foreground, scenery, or aids of any kind—just architecture. You knew at that instant why Henry James, returning round-eyed from a lifetime of exile, had once termed it "the pin-cushion in profile." There was no movement now. For architecture is always still; and its stillness somehow gave a queer effect. One had an odd fancy of enchantment, a sudden hint of some magic word that had stilled guards, courtiers, stable-boys, ladies-in-waiting, and princess, and left the castle towers staring silently across the moat in the pale winter weather. Yet there was movement somewhere; life still flutters in deep gullies at the foot of those enormous towers. For, if that fairy-tale is true, New York is the Unsleeping Beauty.

But as yet she only seemed to wait, politely averted from the dock, as if a thoughtful hostess should allow an interval for new arrivals to dress more suitably for the ceremonious moment of their introduction. Erect herself and plumed like a *débutante* with feathers of white steam, the city waited; and to the eager eye the sight was still related—distantly, perhaps, but still related—to anticipation. One could still believe some of the things that had been written of it. But there the resemblance ended. For New York was utterly unlike its legend.

The same, perhaps, is true of most legendary figures. Lord Tennyson, King Alfred, Pericles, Goethe—how few of these conformed to their reputed image. Cæsar would be a disappointment; even Macchiavelli was only intermittently Macchiavellian; and Napoleon, in a life-time of unsparing effort, rarely achieved the Napoleonic. Indeed, at this very moment, busy (and not too scrupulous) pens point titillating contrasts between the Fathers of the Republic and their less paternal moods, while the energies of England's most ingenious ironist have been required to demonstrate that the Victorians were in the least Victorian. And places are no less deceptive. Naples is Neapolitan, perhaps, and Siena Sienese. But how much of Rome is truly Roman? Florence is barely Florentine; Lucerne is frankly British; and Marrakesh, in bold defiance of tradition, festoons her skyline with unlovely lengths of corrugated iron. For places, like people, limp far behind their legends. Paris (and Bismarck) do their best. But Carcassonne cannot evoke the Middle Ages without the adventitious aid of a Second Empire restorer; Venice, drowning in her own lagoons, was rescued by Mr. Ruskin; and the Renaissance has quite fled from Blois. London, perhaps, alone (and Samuel Johnson) correspond with expectation in their opulent and ramifying solidity. But younger, frailer growths are more deceptive. Perhaps their mythology is just a thought too rich: they may grow into it in time. New York, at any rate was wholly unlike its legend. One sought, of course, to be prepared. But then portraits (by other people) are always so misleading. . . .

The legend is almost painfully familiar. Conceived by generations of bewildered rustics and imposed upon a docile world by seas of print and shoals of celluloid, it evokes the terrifying vision (even poor Henry James had shaken an uneasy pen over "the terrible town") of Manhattan, the devouring city. The Subway seethes; the Elevated roars; the Great White Way performs its appointed function, as the rural moth stoops dizzily towards the blaze. On this stupendous roundabout deadbeats are transferred abruptly from park benches to Park Avenue, while market fluctuations maintain a corresponding service (in the opposite direction) for steel-pawed Wall Street operators, barely visible behind their ranged telephones and swathed, like Laocoon and his unhappy offspring, in the devouring coils that serpentine from the inexhaustible insides of their impassive tape-machines. Opportunity visits young men with firm, attractive profiles in the back bedrooms of apartment-houses; and young ladies secure auditions at the Metropolitan Opera House by singing artlessly over the washing-up on summer evenings, while fascinated gunmen pause in their occupations and even forgers stay their hands to listen.

Vast, brilliant, and a little sinister . . . movies and magazines assisting, I knew the legend of New York. What demented yokel evolved it on what ultimate prairie, we may never learn. Perhaps, indeed, its origins were far from rustic; and when we speculate about them we may be wrong to conclude, from *post hick, propter hick*. For townsmen are often apt to dramatise themselves: it thrills relations from the country. Besides, the greater number of New Yorkers have not been townsmen long. It is, perhaps, the only city in the world that has a peasant population.

I knew the legend, though, and went towards it open-eyed. But the return was empty-handed. For New York, almost alone on the inhabited globe, seemed to have an insufficient grasp of its own legend. Or perhaps it was imperfectly rehearsed.

Something was there, of course—the big policemen twirling clubs, the bright eyes in Baxter Street, the Tombs, and streets that ran through echoing caverns under the Elevated. The sky-signs flashed and rippled, and the buildings soared up towards the day. But where was the light—the fabled bright, Atlantic light? It had gleamed brightly enough outside; but in the city we groped endlessly through mediæval darkness round the base of vast, alarming towers, where kindly voices said gentle, commiserating things about the gloom of London. A citizen of Loches, one feels, might be at home here; and the fable of their light still lingers in those darkened streets from an age before rents and steel-construction had removed the sky to an invisible distance.

That portion of the legend failed me, and the rest was not much more helpful. Ruthlessness was strangely absent. Persons of positively benignant aspect walked the streets quite openly. Even the Metropolitan Museum, terror of European sale-rooms, had a remotely wistful air. I searched in vain for Manhattan, the devouring city. For where New York was most celebrated, it seemed least to be New York. Sometimes, indeed, it gave an odd effect of somewhere else, as of a vast and conscientious pupil moved by dim memories of Paris. Sitting with open ears on the *grands boulevards*, one had frequently suspected that the River Hudson flowed into the Seine. But here and now one learned the Seine to be a tributary of the Hudson. For Paris is often present in the colossal elegances of the shopping district, in its marble facings and the bronze furniture of its shop-windows—a Paris magnified, strangely expanded, and running considerable risks of ceasing to be Parisian in the process. For elegance is awkward stuff to magnify; and the Rue de Castiglione, if sufficiently inflated, may well become Fifth Avenue. Yet Paris was quite unmistakably present, as if massed military bands should render an air composed for solo violin.

Parisian no less (if veering slightly towards Montmartre) a cheerful commonwealth of arts and letters ministers to its enjoyment. There is a wealth of studio gossip, of familiar figures seen at regular tables in characteristic poses, that is strangely alien to the British habit. For Englishmen addicted to these odd pursuits are apt to ply their calling, each in his corner. But New York prefers the more gregarious way that groups dramatic critics at the Algonquin and has its affinities in Paris—the darling Paris of tradition and, I have sometimes feared, of legend. Yet their audience disdains Parisian models. For lacking any touch of that sublime exclusiveness (or is it ignorance?), which excludes from Paris all books not written there and makes of the French the world's provincials, New York confronts the incoming tides of art with a broad gesture of acceptance. Symbolists from Prague, Ukrainian wood-sculptors, performers on unheard-of instruments from recently discovered countries, practitioners of every known and unknown variety of art, even historians from England—each and all are sure of welcome in that vast, expansive heart. For as she waits among the towers of her enormous and enchanted castle, each arriving prince may waken with his kiss the Unsleeping Beauty—happy, happy prince, but slightly, ever so slightly undiscriminating Beauty.

THE PROPHET AND HIS COUNTRY

THE PROPHET AND HIS COUNTRY

THE drummers sit hatted in the big hotel lobby, flanked by a dull gleam of marble and enthroned in vast Renaissance chairs. Rotarians swarm round them on their way to the banqueting-hall, where iced water will circulate in enormous jugs and someone, flushed with this heady vintage, will declaim upon the perfect soundness of things in general. Bells ring; voices call; and bell-boys dart in and out among the throng like swallows. Piled baggage complicates the traffic; and in a corner, where the heavy bronze of Empire mouldings answers the gilt Corinthian capitals of the vast pilasters, highly-trained young ladies deny their correspondence to indignant voyagers because of insufficient knowledge on the part of both (or either) of their own initials. Behind a counter an accomplished man—the linch-pin of this whole rotating world—exclaims at intervals, "Next boy," and releases one more messenger into the whirlpool, bound for the elevators and followed (*longo intervallo*) by his bewildered charges. The traffic seethes like an urban danger-point at rush-hour in this brightly illuminated town within a town. Down in the city lion and unicorn ramp gaily on a coping-stone; one feels that sometimes, a little weary of their grimace, they drop the pose and sit for a while or take a walk down State Street, when the pavements are empty and the silent shops are shut. For it was Boston; and the unwearied drummers still sat hatted in the big hotel.

But it was Boston, though, with its gracious offering of streets that curve, of streets that positively wander among their buildings like remembered streets at home. Boston, perhaps, remembers in the bright New England air, among its little hilly streets of houses. For the town had always a good memory, if slightly inconvenient. Did it not retain a gleam of Cromwell's principles at an awkward moment in the reign of George III? This undulating sea-port, where the north wind comes in over Bunker Hill and the west road runs out to Lexington, made the American Revolution. It heard the angry quaver in Sam Adams' voice and the quick, running footsteps in the winter moonlight as his braves ran for the tea-chests. It caught the sharp note of Howe's musketry; and when an older liberty than freedom from taxation was in question, the deeper voice of Abolition fell on its ear. For Boston has an ear. A shade fastidious, perhaps; but sensitive beyond a doubt. And is it not something that, in the vast receptive organism of the United States, one tiny portion should have the courage sometimes to reject? Malice would hint that Boston's forte is rejection. But malice, as usual, would be wrong. For Boston has never opposed a face of mere negation to the world around it;

and its men of light—the clear New England light—and leading have, each according to his powers, duly lit and led their generation. Yet each retained from his parent, seated a little primly on the hills above the Charles River, one quality that is extremely rare in youthful communities where standards are uncertain and the world tends to take immigrants and immigrant ideas and immigrant books at their face value—the courage to disapprove. Acceptance is so easy. With fewer risks, it often wears a generous air; and its vacancy may sometimes be made to pass for a wide cosmopolitan culture. For what can be more impressive than a catholic awareness of Croat sculpture, Celtic folk-song, and Spanish dramatists? It is the easier path. But Boston, impelled austerely by a Puritan tradition, has often chosen to tread the stonier road of rejection, a harder way since rejection implies a certain poise, some reference to standards, and a process (however summary) of discrimination. Her reward, beyond the little spires and cupolas of New England, was often unjust; since it earned her an unmerited fame for sour-faced disapproval. Integrity is always dangerous; was not Aristides the least popular man in Athens? Yet even the charge of wholesale disapproval is less grave than imputations of its opposite. For the digestion suffers more from excessive catholicity than from a slight fastidiousness: the squeamish man lives longest.

And Boston, at its worst, was slightly squeamish. At its best, it preserved a set of standards in the Great

American Desert; it knew its mind, having a mind to know; and in the universal uproar it retained an ear that could at least distinguish one sound from another. For Boston (I have already said it) has an ear. And when was that ear more sensitive than when a "small vague outsider" floated through the bright New England air, deliciously tormenting father, brothers, sister, nephews, and a grateful legion of attentive readers by a singular gift of indirect allusion—"to avoid naming it straight, but by dint of breathing and sighing all round and round it, to arouse in the reader who may have had a similar perception already (Heaven help him if he hasn't!) the illusion of a solid subject, made (like the "ghost" at the Polytechnic) wholly out of impalpable materials, air and the prismatic interferences of light, ingeniously focussed by mirrors upon empty space"? For that haunting voice hangs, for the eager visitor, on the Boston air. He is for ever hunting echoes of Henry James up the little hills and catching distant gleams of that impalpable refraction. It was positively here that his demure young gentlemen walked genteelly along Back Bay to tea-parties, or his young ladies waited yet more demurely behind their half-drawn curtains for the arrival (always long and often, alas! permanently delayed) of the discreet young gentlemen. One could almost recover the ardours of Dickensians, come three thousand miles to chase phantoms through the Temple. The Dover Road, for them, is not more haunted than Beacon Street for me; and the Common is as thick with echoes as Lincoln's

Inn. So the remembered wraiths come crowding. All his Bostonians pass by, pressing about the visitor as the faint voices of the underworld pressed round Ulysses. Always a little tenuous, those figures seem still thinner as they rise on the Boston air, evoked by memory and the first sight of their actual dwelling-place. But they rise and rise; and the blameless little streets fill with that impalpable Walpurgis. Faint spinsters in pursuit of answers to half-formulated questions; young men at issue with fine shades; and, greatest of his creations, that incomparable elder who returned upon his native country and faced it, like a large slow-spoken Sphinx, with riddles far beyond its comprehension. They were all there on that sedate and shadowy Brocken; and as they danced across the field of fancy, one seemed to catch behind them gleams of a more substantial circle in dinner-table argument with fiercely brandished knives and forks—of the brisk Swedenborgian parent, of Wilky "the adipose and affectionate," a silent, smiling little sister, the electric William, and "covered, like some marine crustacean, with all sorts of material growths, rich sea-weeds and rigid barnacles and things . . . hidden in the mist of his strange heavy alien manners and customs," yet remaining under them all "dear old, good, innocent and at bottom very powerless-feeling Harry."

Not to be denied, they rose on the mind, as the little streets curved in and out, and lion and unicorn ramped on their coping-stone in State Street. The air was bright above the Common, and the big bridges groped across the ice for Cambridge. But the magic seemed to fail, as the long lines of box-cars hooted for switches down by the harbour, where Irishmen were telling Italians how to vote. Its call was fainter still, where the lit street-cars jolted past department stores; and in the big hotel lobby, where Rotary refreshed streamed back to service and the unmoving drummers still sat with their hats on, it fell silent.

QUESTIONS

QUESTIONS

IT IS always easier to ask questions than to answer them: that is why the world in which we live contains more reporters than statesmen. Not that I have much fault to find with the reporters. For, on the whole, they make far less mistakes than the statesmen. But they ask far more questions—and questions, mile after dusty mile of questions, will be the main impression and the most abiding memory of a flurried traveller across the United States (or so many of them as lie between Sandy Hook and the Pacific in an eccentric line that lurched to left and right to take in Texas and Minnesota). For it is always question-time in America.

The questions wait for him at every stopping-place. Ascertaining his whereabouts by some mysterious alchemy, they ring with bland insistence on his room telephone and are shown smartly in to perch upon his trunks and search his soul with their enquiring litany—what are his impressions of the United States? how does he view the last policies (or, perhaps, the last but one) of the State Department? would he favour a censorship of plays, and why? what is the future of the movies, sex, the sky-line, American fiction, opera, the art of dancing, and the wave of crime respectively—or, if he prefers it, viewed as a whole? The scared explorer murmurs the customary polite evasions, to be transformed into resounding truisms for to-morrow's paper. For skilful editing can breathe life into bones whose desiccation would have discouraged Ezekiel himself. But, long before that miracle, he is on the road again and speeding towards the same set of questions, three hundred miles away. Between stations, as he clangs and hoots and jolts his way across a continent, he is tormented by his own private questionings—why, on a luxurious railway-system, is tobacco treated as a secret vice only to be indulged in with every accompaniment of furtive shame? what maniac, drawing names from what stupendous hat, baptised the stations? and what (the supreme mystery of the American continent) are the secret thoughts of those majestic men, who sit about all days with hats on in the Renaissance thrones of hotel lobbies?

But the danger is that these enquiries, which—trivial, if you will—yet constitute his genuine reaction to the new worlds about him, will be submerged in the interrogative tides of commonplace that flood in upon him at every halt. For when he wishes to reflect on Colour and its problem, he is forced to give ready-made opinions on Mexico. His mind fills slowly with impressions upon mass-production; he is just reaching the profound conclusion that mass-production pre-supposes mass-consumption, and that consequently any interruption, however momentary, of the community's ability to consume would dislocate the entire . . . when a fatal courtesy requires him to answer the young man who wants his views on China. And as he kindles to the stupendous vision of the unfolding West, they ask him what he thinks of Mr. James Joyce as compared with Mr. Theodore Dreiser.

These strange rites of initiation are among the most mysterious features of the Dark Continent. Why, in the name of sane and interesting journalism, is it supposed that the opinion of no one in particular (especially on matters upon which he is not qualified to have one) is likely to provide attractive reading-matter? And why does a proud continent refresh itself with the lightest thoughts of every passing stranger who may be pressed into its service as a momentary leader-writer and pontificates gravely upon subjects with which he is imperfectly acquainted? I suppose there is an answer. Most questions have one. But I have never found it, unless it lies in the abiding appetite of this eager race for personal acquaintance. Renowned (and justly) for its taste in *personalia*, it amazes each successive visitor with its glorious intimacy. In an expansive moment it once described the least assured of its explorers as "a Study in Brown . . . a small, dark-complexioned man, with brown eyes, wearing a brown extreme English-cut suit, a tan shirt, brown and tan striped hose, narrow brown pointed oxfords, carrying a dark brown overcoat and hat, and smoking a brown foreign cigarette." Can it be wondered that this blaze of hosier's publicity left him a little dazed?

Yet the staring eye and rudely pointed finger of the paragraphist conceal a human feeling. Sometimes, of course, he is inadvertently ill-mannered, as when a dusty traveller, just off a train, consents to see a caller and is rewarded in the morning paper by a lament over his pitiable declension from the sartorial standards expected (Heaven alone knows why) of all British subjects. But the craving for contacts, which racks the American mind, is a real thing, a survival (possibly) of the age—even now not so distant—when a strange face was an event in the little township and the white tilt of an unfamiliar waggon stirred the farmer (and his wife) to transports of curiosity. This eagerness is the mark of an empty country; and to a European, sunk in that complete indifference to new arrivals which marks an overcrowded continent, the mood is just a little touching.

Less engaging, though equally wide-spread, is the distaste for shorthand. For young gentlemen (and even younger ladies) appear upon such missions, assume the easy chair, make still easier conversation—and take no single note. If a reply should strike their fancy they may (if you are lucky) jot it down in the margin of the newspaper in their hands. But that will be all: no sharpened pencil, no capacious note-book, no mystic curves of Mr. Pitman. The practice, I am well aware, has lofty sanction. For journalistic practice, in a community that has given unusually deep thought to it, discourages the shorthand interviewer. His pencil, it is feared, might distract his recording eye; and lest its flight across the page in hot pursuit of the stranger's opinions should disturb the clear vision of his haberdashery, he rarely uses one. There is, of course, a basis of sound reason for the objection. Since personal impressions are the main desiderata, such things are more likely to be acquired through a watchful eye than with fluent Pitman. For the watcher on the back benches forms a far juster estimate of the Judge than the busy shorthand writer, humped above his flying pencil in the well of the Court. But some of us (vain mortals) are fonder of our views than of our 'personality,' that frankly mythical creation of the morning papers.

Not that the interviewer fails to reproduce them. The miracle is that, with his stub of pencil and his scribble in the margin of a newspaper, he manages so often to secure a reasonable record. Besides, apart from the reporter's freedom to bask in the sunshine of his victim's soul, the victim often has reason to bless his caller's emancipation from the slavery of note-books, since it sets the caller free to talk: I have learnt far more from reporters than they ever learned from me. The conversation of reporters is one of the neglected schools, in which a discerning traveller may learn America. It wears, of course, the weary disillusion common to all young persons under twenty-four who live behind the scenes. But it is singularly informing; and more may be learned about the true temper of local politics from ten minutes with two newspaper-men of opposing parties in a hotel bedroom than from three hours of explanation by local worthies in the course of a conducted visit to the 'high-spots' of civic progress—the sewage-farm, the projected boulevard, and the new

Children's Hospital (Nose, Throat, and Ear). So let not a stranger's voice (himself not unconnected with pens, ink, and paper) be raised in discredit of the American interviewer. He has learnt much from these importunate callers.

And where statesmen complain that their cherished convictions are sadly misreported, his sole grievance is that his own were set down precisely as they were uttered; a good interviewer should have made better ones.

DRY-POINTS

DRY-POINTS

1. Niagara

The trains slid up and down the line from Buffalo behind their big black locomotives; the February sky wore its unlikely blue. Hardly a cloud drifted above Canada; and, deep in its hollow, Niagara uttered its ageless, irresistible challenge to description. First seen as a haze of shattered water hanging on the edge of a vanished river, it reappeared to closer view as a well of solid, sliding green. It stood there in the winter sunshine, fixed in the immobility of perpetual motion. Perfectly still, it took the sunlight on its smooth arch and on the unbroken wall that dropped away into the abyss with the immobile drop of a mountain-side, unmoving as a sleepy top, still as the icicles that fronted it across the hollow and festooned King George's street-lamps on the steep edge of Canada. Its stillness fascinated. Even the unceasing roar had something of the unbroken quality of silence, as the glassy wall stood up immobile in the winter sunshine. But down below it something moved, where the still precipice of sliding water fell sheer away into a boiling fog. A slow Walpurgis of demented shadows eddied up towards the winter sun, mounted, then mounted higher still and fell, steamed up and dropped again into the grey and smoking trough that presently disclosed a tortured, reeling river, last seen a hundred feet above, under a haze of shattered water.

2. *Railroad*

The loose ends of American civilisation flowed slowly past the big Pullman window. Outbuildings leaned unsteadily towards us and were gone. Discarded automobiles rusted reproachfully on scrap-heaps, where the receding tide of progress had left them disembowelled. Small factories almost swaggered by, labelled impressively "Plant No. 1"; the grave enumeration seemed to hint at vast industrial vistas, promptly contradicted by aggregations of the most woeful sheds. Our locomotive clanged the dismal bell, that carries to every British ear a hint of Sunday morning (nothing seems odder to Englishmen than rolling across a continent behind a disembodied Sabbath); and as the tracks wandered uncertainly through the dishevelled outskirts, backyards and building-lots lay all unsoftened in the hard American light.

No one had quite prepared the observer for these two ingredients of his landscape—the immense untidiness that, masked by the world's demurest housefronts, lies behind the trim concrete side-walks of Time's latest birth, and the comforting deliberation of American trains. The last is almost unspeakably consoling. For the European fancy, haunted by its incurable romance upon American subjects, had visions of incredible speed, of big black cow-catchers whirling across receding prairies and ten-foot driving-wheels pounding dizzily over trestle bridges. But the reality was far more soothing, as the untidy outskirts flowed slowly past the window. The wise Pragmatist may warn us against "the most barren of exercises, the making of international comparisons." But in railway trains he warns in vain. For the winter climate provided by the heirs of Mr. Pullman quite precludes the reading of books; even his fellow-countrymen sit in a stupor over comic strips and cross-word puzzles or stare disconsolately out of the window. Smoking brings no relief, except to those prepared to pursue that anodyne on the unyielding seats of a dejected cell furnished with washing-basins and the illimitable conversation of travelling salesmen. So what remains, as the unsweetened building-lots go by and the bell clangs for level crossings, but the barren exercise of comparison?

We droop in our revolving chairs. Below the window, where the ampler telegraph poles of the New World slip past, the steam pipes crack and echo in the mounting heat; and we recall almost with emotion our fading illusions—the speed, the ten-foot driving-wheels, the trestle bridges. Yet American romance is nowhere more persuasive than in railway travel. Trains wear delicious names. "Scouts," "Pathfinders" and "Navajos," redskins of every imaginable celerity, stand throbbing with steam up at platforms; firemen in overalls look down, horn-spectacled and slightly self-conscious, from the tall cabs of waiting locomotives and shift cigar-ends in their mouths; soft Alabama voices gently exclaim "All aboard"; the driving-wheels fly round and grip the rails; and the whole caravan—"Scout," "Sioux," or "Pathfinder"—moves off with a last gleam from the pictorial emblem on its rear-platform. But there romance is ended. For, as the town goes by, it moves sedately; but through the wider world beyond it moves sedately still. The "Raider" (my names and times are inexact, but the impression is clear) ambles across a continent at twenty miles an hour, rising at unusual moments to twenty-five; "Scouts" race behind it—but no faster; and the "Navajo" flutters his eagle feathers with the same gentle pace. Even the terror of the continent averages a genteel forty-eight. This mild progression affords a pleasant shock to Europeans, mesmerised by impressive nomenclature and the legend of American speed. We are so used to catching something more humbly named "the ten o'clock" and whirling into Scotland behind two pairs of racing wheels. The fells above Penrith have seen us pounding down towards Carlisle without an emblem or a name—but sixty miles an hour. How wise the sage Bostonian, who announced that "of all the forms of mental crudity, that of growing earnest over international comparisons is probably the most childish."

Yet even comparisons should be just; and justice, remembering the full horrors of European railway catering, will recall with gratitude the marvels of meal-time on American trains, to say nothing of the more bizarre attractions afforded by the barber's shop, the writing desks "and modish stationery for correspondence," the "latest national weeklies and monthlies in attractive binders, for men, ladies and children," and (for graver moments) "the day's market report off the wires." For the Limited is home-like, as it ambles, with something of a ship's dignity and all a ship's consideration for its company, past the dishevelled outskirts.

Yet it was a relief to find the suburbs so untidy. One had been half inclined, at sight of endless vistas of irreproachable clap-boarded house-fronts, to accept that irritable fling of Mr. Sinclair Lewis at "a savorless people, gulping tasteless food, and sitting afterward, coatless and thoughtless, in rocking-chairs prickly with inane decorations, listening to mechanical music, saying mechanical things about the excellence of Ford automobiles, and viewing themselves as the greatest race in the world." But the untidiness was reassuring. There seemed a chance that *Main Street* was wrong, that Mr. Lewis (that Great Victorian) had denounced his countrymen rather as Mr. Carlyle denounced our own than as truthful eyes observe them. For there is a human quality in building-lots; and ash-heaps are a sign of health. Egypt, we hopefully recall, left us its refuse. So why not Gopher Prairie? What else was Oxyrhynchus and the mound of Tell-el-amarna? Great ages have their ash-heaps; and there is a hope that every ash-heap may have its great age.

So the thoughts rose unbidden, as the last sheds went

sprawling by. Inside the car the expanding steam pipes still reverberated. There was a gentle buzz of talk from the salesmen in the smoker. But our bell was silent now, as we sailed steadily across open country under a winter sky; and big telegraph poles stalked awkwardly across a foreground peopled only by platelayers, muffled and hooded against the cold, with now and then the brilliant smile and ivory eye of America's unsolved problem. A continent flowed by . . . .

3. New York Central

Across the river, where the ice-floes drifted down towards the sea, a line of hills was watching. Faced with brownish cliffs, they seemed to look down a little scornfully. For the Palisades of the Hudson frown, as if conscious of their slightly exaggerated reputation. Yet one should remember that they owe it to eyes accustomed to the monotony of Western plains. They looked, if truth must be confessed, a little tame to travellers fresh from the more tumultuous geology of Europe. For the Old World excels (as one might expect) in the oldest of all decorative arts—the judicious disposition of geological formations to compose a landscape. Happy the continent that has no geological history. Happy, indeed, but less attractive to the eye. For it is the paradox of scenery that its greatest beauties are always ravaged beauties. Scored with the tracks of glaciers, old continents outshine the smooth and uneventful features of their younger sisters; and loveliness, bred in the disordered ruins of dim geological catastrophes, still haunts them. So the Palisades seem slightly tame to west-bound explorers, fresh from Europe. But east-bound, after the featureless procession of the Plains, the eye acclaims them.

That afternoon they watched the ice-floes in the river; and the blocks sailed by, a shade derisive of the imprisoned steamers by the shore. The country lay under the monstrous untidiness of frost all the way from Yonkers to the pointed roofs of Albany. It was a mild thrill, perhaps, to hear the engines hoot across the water to Sing-Sing. But a greater thrill was waiting. For suddenly the jarring brakes had halted us right opposite a single name framed (and how rightly) in gold; and the frame enclosed the blessed word 'Poughkeepsie.' The shocks of New-World nomenclature are rarely analysed. Perhaps too rarely, since more than half the charm of American travel resides in the place-names. What delight in Rolling Prairie; what grace in Miami (until it is pronounced as the indignant outcry of an angry carpenter inquiring for "my 'ammer"); what unquenchable merriment in Ypsilanti. And what nobler introduction to the theme than the railway-line that runs, in geographical delirium, from Poughkeepsie to Rome, by way of Utica and Amsterdam, and then on to Syracuse?

It is absurd, of course, to be affected by such a trifle as a name. Yet familiar names, once mastered, are not easy to dissociate from familiar places; and successive shocks await the European memory on American railroads. Rome was a goods yard; Utica might be searched in vain for any monument to Cato; and it is not easy to respect the mentality that has located Berne and Geneva in the plain of southern Indiana. Yet the system is not without its moments of rare felicity; for Oxford, Wisconsin, lies in wise juxtaposition to Grand Marsh. But perhaps its crowning mercy is the delicious trinity (in three successive stations) of Siberia, Bagdad, and Bolo—the frozen North, the gilded East, and the pale shadow of a half-forgotten spy.

Is it unpardonably frivolous to be amused by such trivialities? Perhaps. Yet one must be kept amused on railway journeys, even while the more solemn portion of the mind admits that names must come from somewhere, that a man has a perfect right to call his town Toledo if he wants to, or even Palmyra. But there is more, perhaps, in the glorious and calculated disarray of American place-names than a mild joke or two. For it provides, in a neat and portable form, an exquisite parable of that New World, which is the Old World taken to pieces, shipped to another hemisphere, and re-assembled in a quite different order to make the United States. In one view, the great American *mélange* consists of all the ingredients of Europe granulated, passed through a sieve, thrown in the pot haphazard, and left (as the cookery books say) to simmer. All the elements are there, with one significant exception. For the French are considerably under-represented in that Gargantuan recipe. If France had been more present in the mixture, who knows what America might have derived from that element, which has often been a light in the European darkness and more than once the binding of the European wall? Small wonder, though, in this grand amalgam where one hemisphere has been poured into another like a trunk hastily repacked, that Batavia should elbow Corfu and passengers for Goshen begin to get their baggage ready at Millersburg.

But I digress. For Rome lay behind us; we were past Oneida now; and Syracuse was coming. Soon we should see it; and as our engine's doleful bell clanged through its streets and past its waiting shop-fronts, we looked eagerly for Archimedes, tracing his circles in the sand.

4. *Waiting-Room*

The barber's pole rotated in its upright glass-case like a demented sugar-stick. That gyrating tricolour almost seemed to call for music; but all its stripes—red, white, and blue—went round and round and up and up in an uncanny silence. Over in the corner a stupendous news-stand offered the Gargantuan fare of transatlantic journalism—Sunday papers a foot thick ablaze with comic strips, local evening journals that were a riot of corybantic head-lines, and bright-coloured magazines alive with stunning blondes or with open-air young men in lumberjacks and braces doing the manliest things all across their covers. These feverish delights were helped out by yet more hectic apples, polished within an inch of spontaneous combustion and ruddy to the point of apoplexy. Assorted candies tempted; strange, highly-coloured beverages waited to be consumed through straws out of little bottles; pencils in stacks prepared to solve their cross-word puzzles for exhausted travellers; and every known variety of chewing-gum stood ranged in order. It was a noble spread; even the peanuts were alluring, and I knew the pecan candy (at 10 cents the highly brittle packet) to be quite irresistible. Remembering the meagre fare of native book-stalls, which suppose the soul to be satisfied with last Wednesday's *Punch* and a piece of ink-eraser, I hung a momentary head.

Random sentences echoed in the great, vaulted roof. Its human contents mostly drooped on the transverse benches, looking a little like the shapeless bundles which composed their luggage and waiting hopelessly for someone to announce their train. Sharp footsteps crossed the stone floor briskly. At a distant counter an endless argument proceeded between a traveller with a sawing, plaintive voice and a young man in check shirt-sleeves, who wore an eye-shade rather jauntily and had his utterance slightly impeded by the last frayed inches of a cigar. The traveller, it seemed, had checked his baggage on some inaudible date from some point equally inaudible on another system. He sawed his way through an interminable narrative of railroad vicissitudes with frequent changes, at the end of which the baggage was not immediately forthcoming. The Company (in shirt sleeves) asked for time. The traveller soared (or, more accurately, sawed) into eloquence, while the Company, only mildly interested, shifted the last inch of the frayed cigar and undertook a little languidly to check up on it. At this the narrative reopened more serratedly than ever; and as the aimless dialogue proceeded, a head or two on the transverse benches turned listlessly to hear, and the words drifted up towards the noble span of the great, vaulted ceiling.

America will be singularly fortunate, if the next civilisation remembers it by its railway-stations. One of the wildest hazards of history is that which dictates to posterity the particular feature by which it recalls a preceding age. Rome, by some accident, is almost all aqueducts in our recollection, Egypt all funerals. We can scarcely imagine the Roman parent otherwise occupied than in building or repairing aqueducts, the Roman young couple walking elsewhere than to the shadow of their favourite arch, the Egyptian relative otherwise employed than in ordering mourning. Such chance survivals cause the oddest misconceptions, the most lopsided reconstructions of the past; and it is a shade disturbing to reflect that we shall lie one day, beyond all opportunity of contradiction, at the mercy of such hazards. Some patient, fumbling excavator will happen on our least considered relics and build the dizziest conjectures on them. They will be hard, durable articles, of course. For all the flimsy things that are most typical of us will perish. Our books will all have gone; so will our pictures (which is, perhaps, as well), to say nothing of our music, briar pipes, arm-chairs, brassies, fishing-rods, window-frames, footballs, and wall-paper.

What remains? Some isolated *cache* of discarded razor-blades will disclose a shadowy presence on the haunted sites of our deserted cities. Or the questing spade will turn up a rusting and congealed accumulation of used gramophone-needles; flushed scientists will pass them reverently from hand to hand, whilst a protracted controversy reconstructs our lives from these imperfect data. One cannot think that, from the information at its command, posterity will envy us. . . . It is an odd reflection, which I commend to archæologists, that we almost invariably misconstrue the past through missing its perishable items. For Rome, which we recall as a grim citadel of imperishable materials, was not all bronze and marble. Yet it is only in our steel and stone and iron that we shall survive.

That fate, undoubtedly, will be ours one day; and when it comes, a well-wisher may be excused for hoping that, for America's sake, it will be remembered by its railway-stations. Better by these, perhaps, than by the writings of Miss Gertrude Stein. Ford cars will perish like the grass; the saxophone corrodes and moulders; and typewriters vanish with the snows of yester-year. So will cash-registers, Kodaks, and bound volumes of the Proceedings of learned societies. But somewhere, I trust, an unborn excavator's hand will lay bare the Union Station. Science, of course, will err (after an unsuccessful effort to connect the edifice with some form of public worship) in supposing that the dim generation of twentieth-century Americans passed their whole lives in catching trains (for the railway-station will perform for them the same misleading function as the aqueduct for Roman life and the pyramid for Egypt). But might they not be pardoned, if they did? For they have such noble places to catch them in. The foreign visitor, indeed, succumbs to this temptation and does very little else. His American life is spent between one vast booking-hall and the next. For him, unnumbered red-caps endlessly recede down lengthening vistas; bells of phantom locomotives clang somewhere out of sight; and the hardy stranger, accustomed to the pioneer simplicity of European travel, parts with difficulty from the massive comfort of the waiting-room, where the barber's sign revolves its tricolour appeal with a flattering suggestion that he is careful of his appearance, the magazines hint softly from their covers that he requires a blonde young lady for the journey, and a book-store offers (subtlest flattery of all) to sell him one of his own books.

5. *Sunrise in Michigan*

It was black night on the empty street outside the sleeping hotel; and a lonely traveller stepped out into the chilly silence, leaving behind him a fine wasteful blaze of electrics and the slow stretching of a drowsy 'bell-hop,' as he faced without exhilaration the gleam of street-lamps on a wet, black street. Somewhere across the road a bright sign exhibited a promise of all-night refreshments, where the explorer found early workmen sitting round a counter on revolving stools and greeting the unborn day with doughnuts, "cawfy," and bisected grape-fruit. Eight minutes later, as the clocks were striking six, the waiting taxi started into the darkness. For it was still black night.

The lit crucifixes of American lamp-standards gleamed down the empty streets. There was a wink of traffic-control electrics, and sometimes a glare from passing street-cars swept through the taxi's dark interior. But soon the city streets gave way to the long pavement of country roads. It was still night; but outside the city it was not so lonely. For the bright eyes of automobiles came swooping up the road towards the town. Its workers were assembling for the day, and each of them sat at his steering-wheel behind his headlights. Lit cars stood waiting in silent alley-ways beside small houses, as the long string of workmen swept down the road in front towards their work. The road was black, rimmed by a mourning border of black fields. But in the sky darkness grew slowly visible—black clouds against a ground of black. Then the clouds grew blacker, as the sky behind them paled into greyness; and the black road turned slowly grey—a grey strip running between black fields that seemed to hold an invisible hint of green. Very far away, behind the half tones of the sky, something put out a broken gleam. It showed the edges of the clouds; it showed the greying masses of the roadside; and some exudation of it stained the grey strip of pavement a dingy white. The world was paling fast, and by its uncertain light a bleached road ran due south across a greenish, brownish country. The swooping headlights lost their magic and become dishevelled 'flivvers.' Tall chimneys stood up against the sky; a bill-board croaked a grotesque (and slightly intoxicated) welcome to "Jackson, City of Action"; and day had come to Michigan.

6. *Tank Town*

Somehow the situation seemed familiar. As I alighted from the tall step of the Pullman, received the last refulgent smile of its attendant darkey, and looked along the train, there was a hint of something dimly remembered. Yet the scene was anything but memorable. A Père Marquette train stood at a station —stood, rather (to be more precise), where a station would have been had anyone thought fit to build one. For a single shed in the middle distance was the sole indication. The waiting train filled the entire perspective, as its tall, polished sides took the level light of a winter afternoon. It hooted huskily; the big cars slid by; and the train receded slowly into Michigan. No other passenger had got out; and I was left standing by the tracks, alone with my small belongings and a vague sense that I had seen it all somewhere else before. The train, a dwindling point now in the rough Canadian landscape, moved deliberately out of the picture; the tracks resumed their interrupted peace; the station-shed, wholly unmoved by the sight of a lonely figure standing forlornly by its baggage, still occupied the middle distance. No one seemed to care; the visible world was utterly indifferent; the . . . . Then I remembered. How many times had I seen movie heroines arrive precisely thus—the big locomotive (with impressive jets of steam); the long line of halted Pullmans; the deferential darkey, as a trim figure comes tripping down the steps; and then the train's departure, and the solitary arrival waiting, a little wistful, by its bag in an indifferent world. It was, of course it was, the recognised approach to life in a small town. In an ecstasy of recognition I almost shaded an eye to catch the last of the big, friendly train with its sympathetic brakeman and removed (close-up) one tear of glycerine.

Not more eagerly did Henry James acclaim, through slowly drifting clouds of circumlocution, some remembered aspect of Newport. For here it was, the indubitable small town of countless slightly sentimental dramas. Its stamp was on the chilly welcome; and (better still) its tank, the authentic tank, was on the sky-line. That ungainly symbol was my final confirmation. How soon, I wondered, would it be before I saw the comic help and her invariable swain (in a hat too small for him)? My eyes would soon be gladdened by the kindly storekeeper gently rocking on his porch, by the world-famous profile worn (in this picture) by a young millionaire from Harvard passing his vacation *incognito* as a farm-hand, and the pursed lips and narrow eyes of those familiar and attenuated figures who would disapprove in corners of my . . . . But I forgot; for I was not the heroine.

Yet the small town was there, plain as its tank, for

any student of the films to recognise. Perhaps the young man, who drove me from the station and assured me in his jolting Ford (it jolted exactly as they did in movies) that I should find "our community hotel" as good as home, mistook me for the heroine. He may, indeed, have been the hero; for his driving was noticeably amateurish. But after that the bright illusion faded. There were no comic loafers; no village prudes whispered in sewing-circles. For small towns in Michigan are not all that Hollywood supposes.

The disappointment passed. But as it died, the traveller was left reflecting on the sad incapacity of art to render nature. That, however, is a large general question; and travellers have little time for general questions. But how far, I wondered, is one particular form of art clouding our minds by persistently misrepresenting life in the United States? Graver pens than mine were already busy with the larger grievance that films are hopelessly misleading to thoughtful orientals; that the white man's darling prestige suffers beyond repair from nightly demonstrations on the screen that State Attorneys have their lapses or that forgers possess hearts of gold; and that East and West can hardly hope to meet, as long as one of the two is left under the impression that white men are mainly occupied in bank robberies, surreptitious courtship, and reprieves. It may be so. It is just possible that Mr. Eugene Chen has vowed himself to the destruction of those unyielding capitalists in white waistcoats who give large parties in the conservatory just to show how rich they are, and that the vamp, her sex's dark reproach, supplies its main motive-power to Swaraj. I doubt it, though. But what I do not doubt is that the films have become, for good or evil (mostly, I think, for evil) the main interpreters of the United States to an interested outer world. We have all learnt America in picture theatres; and it is distinctly unfortunate that we have learnt it wrong.

It is a genuine misfortune, since international understandings rest upon international knowledge; and so long as movie magicians evoke their Djinns and Afrits from enchanted bottles in Southern California, one can hardly hope to know the United States. One enterprising industry persists in circulating a delirious travesty; and if America is misjudged, it has only its own enterprise to blame. That, perhaps, is the vengeance of Heaven upon the block-booking system.

One was left wondering if other forms of art are equally misleading about other countries. Is our own conscience clear? What wells of information do we offer to interested strangers? Looking back from Michigan towards Europe, I could see those homely shores transfigured through a rich haze of opera. One might (in Michigan) be pardoned for concluding that European life consisted mainly of musical processions, in which baritone kings are led out to coronation in canvas cathedrals, or village revels where a singing peasantry carouses from paste-board cups. That is the Continent, of course; and it is notorious that almost anything may happen on the Continent, though I have never found a strong Wagnerian element in German life, and storms in Switzerland are strikingly unlike Rossini's. But is our own country any better served? There is always Shakespeare; and a sudden fear assailed me that the Bard provides a rich mine of misconceptions for the transatlantic student. There are other sources, too, in all of which the English scene is obstinately 'old-world.' Are these the springs at which America drinks knowledge of Great Britain? If so, there is much to be forgiven—even to Big Bill Thompson. For in the travesties that we export there are so many courtiers; monarchs abound; and can we hope to be wholly understood, if we persistently export a picture of British life in which Shakespearean kings move perpetually through a landscape of velvet lawns and moated granges? Does the visitor from Michigan experience, at the sight of bowler-hatted crowds fighting for seats on omnibuses, just such illusions as beset me in his home-town? If so, art is the very worst of all ambassadors; and two continents, known to each other through the movies and Grand Opera respectively, can never hope to meet.

7 *The Haunted Desert*

Half Cumbrian, half Pyrenean, powdered with the last spring snows, the Rockies keep their watch between the Great Plains and the sea. But they were behind us now, and we rolled steadily across a landscape almost entirely composed of pure geology. For the night had wrought a strange transformation. Ourselves were wholly unchanged. We were all there—the patient traveller, the fretful child in Number 8 and her indifferent mother, and the large gentleman from Denver with a Kiwanis emblem in his buttonhole and an unquenchable belief in Buicks for all wayfaring emergencies (enumerated one by one and dwelt upon with loving detail). George, the generic Pullman porter, slept in attitudes of infantile *abandon* or engaged in endless disputations with a visiting colleague—George no less—from the next coach that rumbled with dignity in front of us under the preposterous surname of Begonia (our own was Myosotis). A hopeless vendor still did his best in face of every discouragement to tempt us with candies from the town behind or papers from the town in front; and each of us repelled his advances after our own fashion—the traveller by reading French to show that he was European and therefore immune from such desires, the gentleman from Denver by an uninterrupted flow of narrative. Someone was peeling oranges. For the night had left us quite unchanged; and our little caravan rolled on, an island of indifference, across the changing landscape.

All its contours were lower now. The rich profusion of geology, which would have drawn tears of gratitude from Professor Tyndall, was sinking fast; and no more self-explanatory hills exhibited their strata. The heights were now unlikely hummocks that stirred a faint memory of Sheba's Breasts; and the levels held occasional pastures, where the green was dun and the dun reddish. So we rolled endlessly behind the dreary clangour of our locomotive's bell across the red distances of the desert. For the caravan still rumbled on, traversing the long perspective in a reddish haze, and in the haze the pitiable recollection of Penzance, Arizona. What despairing Cornishman, dreaming of Truro, named this lodge in the wilderness? Did he hear the tide-rip off Land's End on baking nights, when the dust-devils danced before his porch and the hot wind from Mexico breathed across Arizona? He was so far from Looe and the little houses of Polperro. And yet a Cornishman might feel at home in the red desert. For Cornishmen, they say, are sometimes more than half Spanish; and the red desert has a Spanish look. Spain is never very far from the Santa Fé trail. It echoes in Manuelito and Las Vegas; there is a touch of it where the Fathers built their missions; and sometimes a tumbled sky-line hints at the bare hills outside Toledo. One is left with an odd fancy that when Spain carried with her in her conquests her language, art, and religion, she took her landscape too.

So we rolled on across the desert. The gentleman from Denver, his passion for narrative temporarily assuaged, was sleeping; the fretful child, too tired even to complain, drooped inconsolably; and in the corner of the car George shifted his position to dream more easily of a Pullman porter's paradise, where there are no more beds to make and everyone is quite polite. Another caravan pants by and waves a hand from its rear platform. In front of us the rails stretch forward endlessly to California; behind they stream as endlessly beneath the observation-car; and on either side the indifferent desert offers its red distances to our unseeing windows. We have ceased to be a train crossing a landscape and are now a point moving across a map devoid of features. The eye, with nothing to look at, becomes unutterably tired. Even the shimmering delusion of mirage scarcely amuses it. For the prospect is as dull as the world before Creation, a void punctuated at regular intervals by the monotony of telegraph poles.

But the desert is not always empty. Sometimes, a little after sundown, it has a haunted look, an air of frequentation that makes one glad to be in a lit train moving away from it towards the lights of cities. As the day dies, its colour falls from red to grey, from grey to lavender, and from lavender to a dead alkaline-white. Smoky rainstorms hang about its edge. A scurf of desert vegetation streams by the moving windows; and the light fades behind a ridge of hills that seem to owe their tortured outline to long and conscientious study of Doré. A slow storm climbs up the sky like a moving darkness; and in the little wind that runs before it the piñons wave their lonely arms. One feels that in a little while, when darkness falls, they will not be so lonely. For something seems invisibly assembling in the desert. Even the telegraph poles are almost spectral now; and the air is full of evil. For as the night shuts down, the desert is not always empty.

8 *Santa Clara*

'Des pruneaux encore! . . . Jamais de la vie!'
—Tartarin sur les Alpes.

They say that prunes are unromantic. But for me, after that morning, they will always wear the authentic colour of romance.

We woke on *terra firma*. It was not for once the gently undulating deck of the west-bound Limited, whose depressing bell had been my intermittent lullaby nights out of number. The waking eye, accustomed to discouraging encounters with its owner's coat sheeted sepulchrally and swinging slightly on a Pullman hook, incredulously recognised the ampler comforts of a fixed edifice, and closed again. They were still there when it reopened; and it ranged in happy recognition over a solid spaciousness unknown even to west-bound trains. Such, perhaps, were the rare moments of felicity snatched by the Flying Dutchman, when in port for brief, forbidden spells. For the waking sleeper lay, beyond all controversy, in a bed; the bed (so much was plain without undue exertion) stood in a room; his things were scattered round on chairs; there were even tables; drawn curtains hinted at windows; and, perhaps, behind the curtain there were views—views that would positively stand still to be looked at, instead of sliding irritatingly past the pane behind an awkward file of telegraph poles, the unvarying foreground of all railway landscapes. But for a time a more immediate foreground claimed him, where his bed was barred with breakfast—breakfast with marmalade, the ultimate perfection of American hospitality to a British guest. The view could wait.

It waited. But ultimately it could wait no longer. Something invisible behind the curtains called. A faint, isolated note or two of its call was audible in the narrow strip of sunlight just below the window. It must be very light out there; and for a while one lay, vaguely contented by the thought of how light it must be outside and how kind it was of them to send up marmalade for breakfast. But bed, even post-prandial bed, cannot last for ever. The strip of sunlight on the floor grew more appealing every moment; bare feet met the carpet; an arm threw back the curtains; and California flooded in.

The room was full of sunlight now. But who could look behind? A sunlit garden lay below, flowered to distraction, where the tall cypresses, its pacing sentries, had paused to admire their shadows; and its colours melted in the soft Pacific light. That was the foreground. Far away a line of mountains met the sky, their hollows filled with morning shadows and their heights (but did I not promise half California that I would keep their shameful secret?) still flecked with snow. It was the Coast Range, standing up ten miles away to take the morning; and it stood like a wall behind the picture. But the broad canvas flowed more easily towards its background. For, right and left, an open valley spread straight from the window to the distant foothills. Half-way, in the middle distance, the Guadaloupe flowed between its sycamores across the picture. But there was something odd about that plain. Plains should be green, especially sunlit plains in spring-time. It was a sea of orchards; and those level waves seemed green at first—green, if a trifle pale. But as one looked, they paled still further, fading perceptibly from greenish till they blanched into white. For the whole plain was dusted white with plum-blossom; and that incredible valley-floor was carpeted with plums—with (why burke it?) prunes. So, for me, after that morning prunes will always wear the authentic colour of romance.

To meet the Santa Clara Valley suddenly in flower is something beyond the grasp of adjectives and the rich eloquence of railway folders. It is not easy, perhaps it is scarcely possible, to evoke that sunlit picture. Yet if M. Anatole France could believe one of the innumerable holy men with whom he consoled his own wistful unbelief, St. Clara had a well in Italy with power to bring back the past. For he saw in it the mirrored pictures of *Le Puits de Sainte Claire*. But, for me, it is a small and very gracious past that rises on the still waters of my well of Santa Clara—a long dinner-table buried in plum-blossom where Ireland sat serene and smiling, a path that wound up among the redwoods (with a wary eye for poison-ivy), and the still sunshine of California flooding a half-Italian garden in a white valley carpeted with magic prunes.

9 *Grand Canyon*

> *I attempt no description of this combat, knowing the unintelligibility and the repulsiveness of all attempts to communicate the Incommunicable.*—CONFESSIONS OF AN ENGLISH OPIUM-EATER.

The formula is simple. Take the step-pyramid of Saqqara; stain it a dozen shades of red, from brick-dust to a dingy crimson; lay on the colour in great sweeping stripes, five hundred feet from edge to edge and a half-mile across, until it looks like a mountain that has struggled into a giant's football jersey; summon twenty of its fellows in similar attire; set them to watch a river racing angrily a mile below their summits; enclose the watching hills in a gorge a dozen miles across; and you have, if words can render it, the Grand Canyon of the Colorado River. A wise *Opium-Eater* once refrained from a description of the indescribable; and he alone, perhaps, could render (as only opium could conceive) the ranged insanity of that demented landscape. Seen from the sheer edge of a cliff, where the hills of Arizona look nearly into Utah, it began and ended nowhere. That tormented pattern could surely not be final; and one had a sudden uneasy feeling that earthquake had paused for an instant, that the writhing valley might resume its slow convulsions at any moment. It was a crowded valley; for its floor rose up into odd, decapitated summits, where mad mountains groped for one another with discoloured buttresses. The eye was frankly scared—even the modern eye, which can look steadily at mountains; and that disordered scene would have sent the Eighteenth Century, which shrank from their horrid grandeur, sobbing in panic to its bedroom. It had, as one looked down at it again, a queer, unfinished air, as of a Miltonic Chaos waiting for Creation. There was a total lack of meaning in its distorted features; heaped table-lands looked down on nothing; incredible *arêtes* led nowhere. Perhaps it was a storehouse of forgotten mountains, somehow mislaid among the hills. Yet one had a sense that something no less Miltonic had been at work there, carving the hollows, smoothing the steep escarpments, and squaring the mountain-sides. Something, perhaps, had built it in an evil mood to be a parody of Creation. Even where the blind cliffs offered their red, striated sides with fantastic hints of architecture, the resemblances were all pagan—Egyptian pylons riding on Hindu temples, the towers of Babylon crowned with pyramids, and *ziggurats* that ended in unlikely minarets. Somewhere below the rioting red hills an unseen river poured its rapids through a deep grey cleft; and once its thin and angry whisper drifted up from where the Colorado River, sunk out of sight a mile below, raced roaring through the Canyon. There was no other sound; cascades of silent stone lay in the sunlight, watching a slow dance of shadows across the red hillsides; and thirteen miles away the forests of the further rim ruled on the sky a line of level green.

GETTYSBURG

GETTYSBURG

IT HAD been snowing in the night, and the white roofs of Harrisburg looked positively Russian. But a friendly offer of the seventy mile drive was not to be refused, even though Gettysburg would be strikingly unlike Lee's battlefield that snowy morning. As the big car plunged forward and the blanched roads slipped underneath between the sheeted fields, it was not easy to believe that Maryland was only a dozen miles away. Secure behind the rugs, we seemed unspeakably remote from coons in cotton-fields. Yet Mason and Dixon's Line was over the next hill; and, in the sloping fields between, the fate of Mason, Dixon, Line, cotton-fields, and coons had been determined in three days of intermittent gunfire and promiscuous gallantry.

We looked across the shrouded country and thought a trifle ruefully that it could hardly correspond that morning with the sunlit Seminary Ridge, Peach Orchard, Round Top, and Wheatfield of '63. For Gettysburg had been a July battle; and one should visit battle-fields, each under its appropriate sky—Waterloo at a rain-sodden midsummer; Wagram (as once I did) in the breathless heat when the Viennese are gasping for *Eis-kaffee* and tree-shadows lie like tall pencils across the white Aspern-Essling road; Culloden in raw Highland mist; Sedan under a leaden sky; and Metz in the still autumn days that watched Bazaine between the dripping trees, as the leaves fell and the last eagles of the Empire drooped miserably towards surrender. So it was not to be hoped that Gettysburg would wear its own aspect on that snowy February day.

But there were compensations. For the snow, which hid the ground, would hide the monuments as well. I speak without irreverence; since reverence is rarely assisted by those sorrowing divinities and foot-soldiers shouting silently in stone, with which the monumental art loves to embellish scenes of glory. Mounted generals raising perpetual bronze *képis* do not aid the fancy; strained gunners (in bas-relief) are equally unhelpful; and imagination frankly quails before the larger carnivora in post-prandial attitudes. On a deserted battlefield one gropes for echoes; and a too noisy allegory may disturb the air. I was never nearer to the past, I think, than once in the silent valley that lies between the two smooth ridges of Valmy. Sculpture had admirably neglected her opportunities; and I was perfectly alone, since the other sightseers, misled by an extremely small-scale map of Mr. Belloc's, had started in the wrong direction. But the ridge was there in the still sunshine, where the Republic faced the kings; and there, confronting it, was the bare slope where the stiff Prussian infantry made their uncertain movements, and the green hollow in between where

Goethe, most glorious of all war-correspondents, had walked under the noisy arch of that erratic barrage, reflecting that a new world was coming to birth—or so he remembered several years later, when it was considerably easier to be impressed by '92. It was quite silent when I walked there; but the silent emptiness was filled with sound and movement—with Kellermann immensely plumed, Dumouriez looking a little anxious, and the crash as the fired caissons went up in smoke behind the startled French. For one can fill the void, where memory has space to spread its wings and no distractions step between the watcher and the past.

But crowded fields are harder to recover; and Gettysburg is distinctly crowded. Piety has marked the post of every unit through the three days of fighting. Where the record consists of little field-guns, it aids the memory since they are the guns of '63; but in its other forms it almost seems to hinder. We can scarcely recall events that are so elaborately remembered for us. Thus may a predigested meal defeat digestion. Besides, the whole *Denkmälerei* effectively destroys the fine uncertainty of facts, to which alone dramatic happenings owe their drama. So as Pickett advances on the predestined futility of the 'High Water Mark Monument,' his columns seem to move rather across the page of a text-book than across a field. Thus can commemoration paralyse our groping memory.

There is a wealth of sculptured effort; even the South has broken silence. And as I saw it draped in snow that morning with the white sheets drawn closely up to each military chin, it had an odd air of a drawing-room wrapped up with care for a long absence of its owners. Indeed, its owners were all absent—or very nearly all—sixty-four years away. So trim and decorous a place could not be haunted. But as I watched, it was still waiting in its sheets; and one day, perhaps, they will come again.

Yet something hung even on that winter air. There was a hint, above the bronze and marble and the neat winding walks, of a tall figure rising to half its height, a twist of paper crumpled in a bony hand, and then a dragging utterance—"Fourscore and seven years ago. . . ." For some speeches echo louder than a gun-shot.

THE PLATFORM

THE PLATFORM

'Where are you going to, my pretty maid?'
'I'm going to the lecture, sir,' she said.

—OLD SONG.

HOW vividly it all comes back—the slight constraint that settles on the company, as lunch draws to a close; the coffee ordered rather quickly and refused by the speaker with the feeble witticism that it might keep him awake; one or two prescient committee-members rising suddenly to "get good seats in front"; a kindly introducer bearing down, full of consideration and his opening remarks, to ask the lecturer if he prefers to compose his thoughts in solitude (I always wondered how many of my predecessors had answered in the affirmative out of a base desire to impress—for there is something undeniably impressive in the thought of a lecturer alone in the presence of his Maker); and then the slightly uncertain journey down unfrequented corridors towards the back of the building, with a sudden view of the audience seen in profile, row after row, through a half-open door; a dark stumble up the three—the invariable three—invisible steps that end upon the stage; a blaze of lights; the uncertainty which of two large, uncomfortable chairs to sit on; a vague sea of faces; and the scattered applause that greets arriving speakers.

These, carefully recalled from the dim vaults of memory, compose the almost unchanging prelude of a lecture. There may, of course, be minor variations. Sometimes it was at night; and then the opening scene is set at an unnaturally early dinner instead of lunch. Perhaps a friendly Faculty dined in a common-room; but when rational men would settle down to talk their pipes away, the entertainment ends in the same constraint, the same dreadful consciousness of an impending lecture (for lectures, like tornadoes and other convulsions of nature, are invariably preceded by an uncanny silence). Or a hospitable committee meets at a neighbouring hotel. The meeting, after the first embarrassment of introductions, is delightful; but its close is shadowed by quick glances at watches, the furtive departure of an active secretary to "make sure that everything is all right," and the rapid journey of "two blocks"—always (I know not why) two blocks —with glimpses on the street of happy, happy people who are not going to the lecture.

But the lecturer, unhappy mortal, is always going to the lecture. No escape for him. Few can realise how deeply he envies those apologetic diners who rise at the coffee to explain, with copious regrets, that a previous and ineluctable engagement calls them to the opera or to a Philharmonic Concert. For in all well-ordered communities there is a Philharmonic Concert on the same evening as the lecture. I have arrived at the same moment in the same hotel as the performing orchestra itself, checked in between the second fiddle and the third trombone, and listened through an afternoon to their melodious exercises—the horn competing with the gay bassoon, each in his bedroom. So, after that rich foretaste of musical delights, when my embarrassed fellow-diners rose with apologies to pass their evening with Bach and César Franck, how I envied them. For the lecturer is condemned to pass his evenings with himself.

Yet he is not quite alone. For even lecturers have audiences; and in their company the most industrious speaker may learn far more than he can ever hope to teach: he may even (I write in all humility) learn to speak. True, the opportunity is not invariably taken. For the lecture-platform overflows with Strong, Silent Men, faced with the apparently insoluble problem of keeping on talking for an hour and overcoming their invincible repugnance to articulate speech by the most desperate expedients. Some range about the platform like caged lions; some hover insecurely on its very edge and alarm nervous occupants of front seats with the terrifying prospect of receiving a lecturer in their laps, as well as in their minds; and some bludgeon their hearers into a merciful unconsciousness with the studied brutality of a typewritten discourse heaped menacingly in front of them and diminishing as the pile of read manuscript grows—oh! so slowly—under the reading-lamp. Being myself humane, I am always on the side of the audience. I hope that they will win. Have I not suffered agonies of suspense from learned men, whose speech was hopelessly impeded by their learning, as they incited drooping rows of listless hearers in a college lecture-room to "come . . . mnyumm . . . to another aspect . . . mnyahh . . . of the problem . . . mnyum-mnyahh . . ."? Yet the audience at a public lecture is less deserving of our pity. It has only itself to blame: there was no need for them to come.

They have their reasons, though. For some (and these, I believe, compose the vast majority) have come to learn; others, less to be respected, are there to see the speaker. They are the sightseers of literature, eager to view the inadequate little man or the imposing lady whose writings they have long enjoyed in private—and there is, I suppose, a certain satisfaction to be derived from watching a novelist with an output like Niagara struggling for his next word. The lecture-platform may, for all that I know, be the novel-reader's revenge, a Freudian 'compensation' for the deluge of the written word sought in the halting utterance of the lecturer. But if practice can make perfect, there is small excuse for any lecturers to remain inarticulate, when at last they turn their faces towards the comforting silence of home after the endless solo of a lecture-tour. For they will have travelled several thousand miles to the monotonous accompaniment of their own voices. That music will pursue them through every hour of their extremely crowded days, from their rising up to their lying down—and even there, perhaps, they will hear it answering the telephone to explain their deepest convictions in reply to journalistic questions.

They will hear it lecturing, of course, in mornings, afternoons, and evenings. And between lectures they will catch its doubtful melody at every meal where the company consists of more than six. For perfect hospitality seems to proceed upon the somewhat unsound assumption that lecturers like making speeches; and they will have made them with the coffee at the end of every meal, with the solitary (and merciful) exception of breakfast in bed. For a lecturer will learn to dread the words "We have with us to-day. . . ." So he has no excuse for not knowing how to speak, when a whole continent unites to teach him.

But if he can keep his eyes as wide open as his mouth, he may learn a far more valuable lesson. For as he views the long procession of his hearers, all along the road from the Great Lakes to San Francisco, he is in the way of learning more than most travellers. The eager tourist in a new country can always see with a minimum of effort what are termed 'the sights.' Museums and picture-galleries fly open at his approach; ruins offer themselves conveniently for his inspection; cities expose their public buildings; and legislative assemblies tempt his hearing with the delicious notes of their melodious proceedings. These lessons mastered, the industrious visitor may have secured a sound grasp of the externals of almost any nation. But the nation itself remains a mystery. The shopping crowds, the other people in the train, the worshippers in the cathedral are still as dark to him as if he had remained at home and read accounts of their mysterious and remote proceedings in the newspapers of his native country. He sees, of course, the hats they wear, the inexplicable clothes they buy; he tastes the extraordinary food they eat. But their lives, their interests, their minds remain impenetrably closed to him. That is precisely where the lecturer gains his advantage. For as he moves about, commanded by the inexorable schedule of his engagements, he penetrates more deeply than any tourist, sees more than connoisseurs in picture-galleries, and secures a record unavailable to the most industrious Kodak. He may shirk 'the sights'; bad fortune (or good luck) may bring him to every museum ten minutes after closing-time; and the bolts of cathedral doors may shoot noisily in their rusty sockets as he approaches. But he has seen something far more instructive than mummies, Vermeers, or rood-lofts; for he has seen the ordinary man, that most secretly preserved of national sights.

No stranger, of course, can ever see a nation, or even a tithe of one. But he may, if he is lucky, follow a route that cuts a section through a whole community and, if he is moderately observant, form some picture in his mind of the strata that lie on each side of his little mine-shaft. His journey, if sufficiently long and diversified, may well be such a shaft, sunk through the various layers that compose the nation. For it may take him (as mine took me) through the upper layers of the higher education, by way of each successive grade of university and school, to the most fascinating stratum of all, where the ordinary mortal, his education done, stands ranged in due order from the Eastern States to Texas, up into the North-West, and out to the Pacific. That is the finest stratum for the social geologist, if he keeps his eyes about him and his hammer ready for specimens. It is the truest form of sight-seeing that America can offer. For the leading 'sight' of the United States is not the White House or the Grand Canyon, but the ordinary man.

The first discovery that any lecturer will make on this important topic is that the ordinary man is not the ordinary man at all—but the ordinary woman. For his hearers are, in a vast preponderance, feminine. Even his evening fixtures draw a distinct majority of women, though he is not himself a matinée idol or even a novelist announced to discourse on those topics of the heart, in which novelists are believed to enjoy a mysterious competence. Men will be there, of course, but only sparsely present—a shade apologetic in their air and in just sufficient numbers to relieve a nervous lecturer of the alarming exordium "Ladies" in favour of the more habitual "Ladies and gentlemen." Recalling all the rows of friendly faces that passed before a slightly embarrassed eye in its long pilgrimage from east to west, one is confronted (like Don Juan in a memorable scene) with a vision of remembered ladies —though I hope their faces wear a less reproachful look. Memory gives back to me row after row of listeners, at all times of day and in every variety of climate. Sometimes the snow was deep outside; sometimes the sun was shining with an irritating emphasis upon the absurdity of keeping folks indoors on such a day. There was an afternoon at Pasadena. . . . Halls varied; there were cosy meeting-rooms, halls with deceptive echoes, vast theatres where a listless stage-hand flicked on the footlights, and one depressing auditorium, brownish in colour and admirably adapted for use between lectures as a morgue, but with a stage set by some divine ineptitude for a street-scene in *Romeo and Juliet*—I can still recall the sense of inadequacy with which the lecturer and his introducer shambled across that background of Verona in their black evening suits, the hunger for a cape to swing, and the unsatisfied craving for a sword. But one quality united all the listening rows in every hall: they were almost all feminine. One excludes colleges and schools, of course, where the attendance hardly counts in such a calculation for the cruel reason that it was—I blush to record—often compulsory. There remains that vast aggregate of audiences which were entirely feminine, because the occasion was organised by a Women's Club, and the mixed audiences at public lectures, where the men were hopelessly outnumbered.

One is left speculating on the significance of this odd balance of the sexes. Lectures are dull enough; but they are surely not more forbidding to male than to feminine ears. Yet the indubitable fact remains that women come to them, while men remain away. I make no comment on the absence of the American male: we have been taught to think of him as deep in more absorbing occupations. Besides, I entertain no doubt that, given a similar occasion, the British male would be quite equally, if not more, absent. But, then, the lecture forms no part (or only an infinitesimal one) of the British scheme of things. One would stare round-eyed at any subject of King George, aged more than twenty-one, who said in response to questions that he was "going to the lecture." And no attraction, however unusual or sublime, will suffice to get him there. The announcement of a course to be delivered by the Archangel Michael on his experiences in the Holy War—in the Albert Hall, of course (where else would an Archangel lecture?)—would almost certainly find him lecturing to empty benches. For England does not go to lectures. The British male would not be there. But neither would the British female. There lies the impressive contrast. For the multitudinous lecture-goers of America are almost all women.

It is a phenomenon worth analysing further. However ungallant it seems to pass one's hostesses under the microscope, one may pursue the investigation. Where do they live? What kind of people are they? If lecture-going were just a feature of small-town life, one would be inclined to discount its significance. For in small communities, where the stir is slight and the picture-houses only change their programmes once a week, anyone might be excused for going to a lecture. In such instances attendance would not point to anything more significant than a desire for change, a mild hope of entertainment sure to be rewarded by the sight of a strange face and the sound of a still stranger (because so often an English) voice. But the lecture, as a part of the life of American women, is by no means confined to small towns. I have seen eager assemblies in large cities richly provided with every means of distraction for their citizenesses. What, then, is the meaning of them?

One pauses, slightly baffled. Such assemblies, consisted, in the experience of one explorer, of almost every type—young women fresh from college, ladies in middle life, and comfortable elders. Only one element was almost uniformly absent; for the presence of young mothers, deep in their household worries, was something of a rarity, though even that was not unknown. What, one is left enquiring, draws them to the lecture? I am half inclined to think that one factor, which Englishmen may be forgiven for overlooking, is the wide diffusion of university education in the United States. There are a little under six hundred (to be precise, 588) American universities and colleges, with a student population of approximately three-quarters of a million. This mass is not a stationary body; but the stream, constantly renewed at the springs of each new generation, flows out steadily into the community. The men proceed into their various callings, and any appetite for information that college may have stirred is rapidly submerged in the new ardours of their necessary occupations. The law absorbs them; real estate excites; lumber and hardware exercise their faculties—until, when the long day is done, the male, for all his college training, has become the Weary Titan who demands an unexacting evening with his radio, a cross-word puzzle, or a musical play. But the college women? Their fate is very different. For a year or so—longer, perhaps—they live at home unmarried. During this interval a lecture may reasonably appeal as a pleasant means of passing time away. There is still a vague desire to learn; the lecture may lead somewhere new or may continue something half-learnt in college. That feeling, I think, accounts for the presence of one's younger hearers. Then comes marriage; and the home performs for women the same absorbing functions as a man's profession. That is why men and young married women are so largely absent from the lecture-hall. But families, as time goes on, grow up; the home ceases to be an all-absorbing occupation; and the woman is left with leisure on her hands. That is the second stage at which the announcement of a lecture draws her. It seems to beckon with a faint memory of lessons half-learnt, ten, fifteen, or twenty years before. So she goes, unlike her husband, to the lecture, a willing victim of the lecture-habit.

A more delicate inquiry opens. What is the value of the habit? Does the audience that comes bring anything away? A lecturer may be excused for blushing slightly, before he faces that essential question. But the value of his performance does not depend entirely on himself. For it is necessarily restricted by the universal limitations of all lectures. An hour of talking gives him time to utter about eight thousand words—say, four and twenty pages. But the looser texture of the spoken word, with all its repetitions and its emphasis, compels a speaker to proceed far more leisurely than he would with his pen in hand. So his eight thousand words of lecture would probably compress, if written down for printing, into fifteen pages, which a reader could easily absorb in half an hour. So the lecture-audience is, in point of time, a loser. That is to say, it could acquire more knowledge in a shorter period if it stayed at home and read a book. But would it? That question embodies the main (and almost the sole) defence of lectures.

But the lecture is a comparatively worthless thing, if its effect is ended when the audience troops out and the lecturer goes back to his hotel. He may have uttered his eight thousand words and imparted his fifteen pages of information. But unless some, at least, of his hearers are inspired to read a little further on the subject, his effort has been largely wasted and he has been little more than a respectable distraction—a blameless movie or an innocuous play. For the lecture must, if it does its duty, serve as an incitement to reading; and if the more listless members of the audience employ it merely as a substitute, their time—as well as the lecturer's—has been very nearly wasted. That is the haunting fear which shadows every smiling figure that stands acknowledging the mild applause in which his lecture ends. It would be less, I think, if lecture-programmes were less richly diversified. For how can any speaker hope to set his hearers reading history by an hour's talk, if someone a week before has entertained them with "Child Life in Armenia" and they are to listen a week hence to "Bird-lore" with vocal imitations? But that problem is for lecture-committees to solve (with their diverse constituents to please), and not for lecturers. Those harassed mortals can only say their piece, listen to politely murmured thanks, sign copies of their published works, and slip away to their hotels—the Flying Dutchmen of contemporary education, commercial travellers of culture.

STATE LEGISLATURE

STATE LEGISLATURE

FIRST FLOOR: *So wot could it was?*
SECOND FLOOR: *Hmmm—wot could it wasn't?*
—POPULAR CLASSIC.

THE war memorial in the square outside looked, at the first glance, a trifle overcrowded; and, it must be confessed, that noble pedestal was distinctly populous. For its upper reaches were a joyous riot of allegory, where eagles soared and suspended ladies of heroic size made promiscuous awards of wreaths. Our kind conductor kindled the wildest hopes with his unwitting intimation that one of the figures wore "suspenders." That word, so innocent to American ears, is replete with dark significance for Europeans. Had some bronze Victory, we wondered breathlessly, adopted unusual precautions? Was this a sculptural rarity, worthy to rank with the gold *pince-nez* worn for so many years by the late Friedrich Krupp (in bronze) outside the Yacht Club at Kiel? Alas, it signified no more than that some victorious soldier on the lower tier wore braces: it seemed a wise precaution. For in that riotous procession of returning warriors anything might happen. Their homecoming was more than a little complicated, since it appeared on closer scrutiny that they had returned from four distinct (though almost equally victorious) wars a hundred years or so apart. For the City Fathers, with a wise economy reminiscent of that frugal village which combined its war memorial with the victims of a lifeboat accident, had amalgamated on one glorious pedestal all the battle-honours of the Republic. Each of its four appointed wars was there—the Revolutionary, War of 1812, Mexican, and Spanish-American. After this triumph of deft condensation it may be conjectured that they were left slightly baffled by the inexplicable malice of Providence in permitting a fifth war to burst upon them in 1917. For one can hardly add a fifth side to a four-sided monument. So the civic mind was sadly bewildered by fresh problems of commemoration; peristyles and pylons danced in imagination before its anxious eye; and it was haunted by a doubt, due to a slight defect in its classical education, as to what one put inside a cenotaph.

But though we lingered in the shade of that stupendous cairn, the object of our quest was less æsthetic. Open hands had met us at the station with a kindly offer to fill our day for us; and the afternoon, it seemed, was to be filled with the State Legislature, that august *revenant* which appeared within its marble halls once in two years and legislated for six delirious weeks. Since it legislated for thirty thousand square miles of farming land, about a quarter of the size of France, we were prepared to see it with respect. Besides, it was a State of spirit. Had not a sprightly leader-writer in a neighbouring city observed that it was "proud because it has a governor in the penitentiary. . . . It also has Wiz Stephenson of the Klan in there and has walled him in as tight as possible." So we approached its Areopagus with due respect, walking delicately over the chess-board marble of its outer courts.

The House was in a gentle buzz of session. To eyes accustomed to the ranked adversaries of Westminster or the horse-shoe sweep of Continental Chambers, there is inevitably something a little unimpressive in those legislatures where all the members face in the same direction, sitting at little desks. For the arrangement lends to the most adult Parliaments an unexpected air of the schoolroom; one almost looks along the file of bowed shoulders for a black-board, and half expects someone to come in and give them a half-holiday. That afternoon, however, work was in full swing. A mildly conversational assembly was legislating, at the rate of about a Bill every sixth minute, for its three million subjects. One had a sudden vision of the beneficiaries of this legislative energy—of the local lawyer noting up his law-books at fevered speed, the local administrator overloading his congested margins with a tangled fringe of novel duties, the local policeman staring at the mounting spate of his fresh functions in dazed policeman's admiration. Slightly dazed ourselves and deeply admiring, we were led up to Mr. Speaker, who faced the assembly from his dais. A gracious hand waved two astonished visitors to seats beside the throne; and seen from that comfortable vantage-point, the stream of legislation flowed swiftly past. Soothed by the incomparable lullaby of eloquence, we suspected nothing. There was a sudden pause, provoked by Mr. Speaker's hammer soundly rapped on the stone slab in front of him, as he invited the assembly to 'meet' the young ladies of some inaudible academy, present at their deliberations. A sudden fringe of heads appeared along the rim of a distant gallery; and the assembly rose and 'met' them. We were still unsuspecting, when he beat his slab again and asked the House—to our increasing horror—to 'meet' the unworthiest of its spectators. That nervous auditor, having observed the ritual, arose; and a courtly Legislature rose with him. But when he hoped to sit again, the Speaker's whisper in his startled ear directed him to speak. As flight was shameful, he remained—and spoke. But the full terrors of a Legislature's hospitality were still unsuspected. For the Speaker rose once more and, indicating that their guest from England had a wife, invited the assembly to 'meet' her also. Once more the alarming rustle of legislators rising politely to their feet; once more the spectacle of an embarrassed guest smiling uncertainly from the dais, as she 'met' her hosts. Still insatiable, Mr. Speaker demanded one speech more; and since Speakers must be obeyed even by lady visitors, speech was forthcoming. A member covered the family confusion with a word of charming welcome introducing, by way of figurative ornament, one of the pigeons which flapped unaccountably about the hall and was momentarily dignified, for symbolic purposes, as the authentic Dove of Peace. The incident was closed, recorded duly in the Minutes of that august assembly. Such are the happy dangers that lie in wait for rash visitors to Legislatures. A notice might, possibly, be posted in the hall to warn them. But then we should have missed a happy meeting.

THE UNMELTING POT

THE UNMELTING POT

THE preacher's text is large and printed in bold characters between the rank air of the stockyards and the steely purity of Lake Michigan. And the sermon? Let us be clear about it. This is not a reasoned appraisal (with race-maps and statistical appendices) of the race-problem in the United States. To solve that—and it is solved, on an average, four times a week—would be to write the last word upon the American past, present, and future; and last words in history are not written by sensible historians. The golden rule, as Mr. Chesterton observed in a rare lapse from the dogmatic, is that there is no golden rule. A wise Emperor once restrained an impulsive minister with the sage remark, *"En politique il ne faut jamais dire 'Jamais'"*; and students of the United States might well observe the caution. For in America anything may happen. So why speculate about it? A cool agnosticism is by far the safer course. Avoid decided views, and you may be able to face posterity with a bland "I told you so!" But thought cannot be altogether silenced by these unheroic counsels. Besides, it is dull (as well as draughty) to keep an open mind. So hurried travellers rush in where natives fear to tread; and a random drive from the Loop to Cicero and back again may well provoke random reflections. These, then, are offered with all due reserve; inset, a portrait of Chicago.

That daughter of the West sits, if so stationary a verb is applicable to her pose, beside her slightly inadequate river and looks out across fifty miles of lake, while the north wind comes swooping down from Canada four hundred miles away. Her poets, as perverse as poets in gentler climates, linger affectionately on her smoke. They love to grime their goddess and to put smuts on her nose. So the scared traveller had half expected some stupendous lake-side Stoke-on-Trent, barely visible beneath its smoke and lit by the intermittent glare of blast-furnaces. But one can see now that the legend of Chicago's murk was a mere repartee. For New York is universally believed to be extremely light—and Chicago is nothing if not different. Truth must be told, although one would not willingly hurt a single feeling on Michigan Avenue (or even in the City Hall); and it must be confessed with grave reluctance that west-bound trains draw into a tall city, full of light.

There is a difference, though. For the visitor is nowhere haunted in Chicago by those echoes of somewhere else that stir his memories of Europe in certain American cities. There is no note of Paris in the Chicago air, no hint of England; since that robust child does not 'take after' any of its highly numerous parents. Perhaps she is a little too much the *fille du régiment*. The city looks, indeed, towards the east;

but when Chicago looks eastwards, it looks across Lake Michigan, not (Mayor Thompson will agree) across the Atlantic. For here is an American city that is just trying, trying hard, and even trying sometimes a little truculently to be an American city. And how admirably it succeeds. Even civic pride may be forgiven its worst excesses, when it has something to be proud of; and what citizen could walk between the shop-fronts of Michigan Avenue and his gleaming lake without a sinful pride? That, surely, is a half-street worthy to stand in the choice company of the world's half-streets —with King's Parade, and Piccadilly urbanely overlooking its Park, and Princes Street where Edinburgh Castle stares grimly down into the shop-windows. There is no need to swagger about Michigan Avenue; for that stately profile easily compels the praises it deserves.

The tall façades along the lake seem to look nobly out to sea across the intervening ash-heaps. One was a little puzzled by that sudden interlude of ugliness between the calm and regular features of the boulevard and the bright splendour of the lake. For a No Man's Land of holes and heaps and rubbish intrudes, like a line of dust-bins between a sumptuous auditorium and a lit stage; and visitors are pardonably baffled by that devastated area, by the protracted and not yet successful efforts of the gigantic daughter of the West to complete her toilet. One was a shade embarrassed by the encounter, as though a nervous traveller should come on a large (and undeniably attractive) young woman doing her hair up in the corridor, her lovely mouth still full of pins. Here is a city that can erect an office-building forty storeys high in three months. Yet its lake-front, the brightest jewel in its civic crown, remains a wilderness of stone-heaps. One hates to feel (but what other answer is there?) that private profit can move mountains, while public works wander uncertainly through a labyrinth of railway-franchises and municipal contracts.

But there are consolations. For official ingenuity has found a way to gratify the sense of beauty without undue exertion or expense. Along the scarred and battered front, that is sometimes more reminiscent of bombardment than town-planning, a line of billboards announces the projected embellishments on the simple principles of Elizabethan scenery. One had seen actors in unduly scholarly revivals vainly endeavouring to perform with dignity before a clothes-horse simply ticketed "This is a castle"; and the same chaste expedient compels Chicago to trail its incomparable robes of beauty across a stage where, in default of other scenery, we read "This is a foot-bridge." Hardly just to a sublime performance, the device applies the principles of M. Coué to town-planning and might, with advantage, be employed in other contexts. For how deep our thanks, if memorial committees were to hold their pious hands and substitute for unlovely heroes prancing on unlikely steeds a simple notice-board bearing the chaste inscription "This is General Bloggs."

But larger questions lie behind the regular beauty of

Chicago's lake-side profile. For the whole riddle of the American future is asked (though scarcely answered) by the alien litter of Maxwell Street. What is the eventual meaning of those hundred thousand Poles, these streets alive with the -aks and -eks of exiled Bohemia, the sleek Italians, the demure and polysyllabic Greeks, and the solid half million Germans? Here, within the city limits, is the second Czech, third Swedish and Norwegian, fourth Polish, and fifth German city in the world. It prints newspapers in a dozen languages and worships God in twenty. One thing is obvious: the fabled melting-pot is not yet heated to a point at which the elements consent to fuse. For in Chicago, if the evidence of the streets may be believed, the Pole is still a Pole, the Czech remains a Czech, and the Croat no less a Croat than on the day he passed the Ellis Island turnstiles. If this is a fair sample of the American *mélange*, Europe is not yet blended, though the multiple ingredients of that stupendous broth lie scattered in hopeful disarray on the kitchen table.

One odd result has followed. For though the amalgam is not yet constituted, some chemical action has taken place within the various elements. It is, in one aspect, disturbing; since transplantation seems to have changed certain, at least, of the European breeds—and hardly for the better. One should not overrate the crime-wave. Yet it is barely possible to read the papers or to see a slant-eyed, brownish-yellow house-front in Cicero, freshly sprayed with machine-gun bullets, without an odd reflection that the Italian as we know him seems strangely different from the "Wop" encountered by the American police. Harmless in London, mildly addicted to the knife and *crime passionnel* at home, he soars in the bright American air to novel heights of wickedness. What is the cause? One wonders whether wide economic opportunity is not too much for weak European characters. Or can it be the climate? After all, it was on this spirited continent that our blameless Nonconformity flowered unforgettably into Salt Lake City. I can do no more than indicate the riddle—and ask policemen in Soho if they could recognise their dark and smiling friends in the Italian gangsters of an American city. For the alien, it seems, is often strangely corrupted in the new country of his choice. Perhaps he wants to be: that may be why he goes there.

But one would be wrong to see Chicago only as a vast alien welter. For, "gigantic, wilful, young," she is nothing if not American, a young relation of Walt Whitman. That authentic note may be heard more clearly here than anywhere in the United States. New York seems almost Parisian by comparison; looked at from Illinois, Boston seems a cathedral town and New Orleans a Franco-Spanish port. So Mayor Thompson knew his business when he chose to fight a municipal election on the far from municipal slogan, "America First." Mayor Thompson is, indeed, a portent. His more apologetic countrymen tend to wave him aside as something unfit for foreign eyes; but they cannot altogether explain him away. Here is a fantastic booster in a cowboy's hat who swept into office in the second city of the Union by a majority of more than eighty thousand votes. The issues were mainly irrelevant; the causes I leave to local scientists to explain, merely appending (in mute awe) the ecstatic diagnosis of one supporter:

"His election is a clear victory for the candidate of the people. Highbrows and lowbrows alike were hostile. Thompson lost in the silk-stocking districts and in the famous First Ward, controlled by 'Bath-house John' Coughlin and 'Hinky Dink' McKenna. He won by the vote of the average citizen, whose Mayor he proposes to be."

A profounder student drew the more interesting conclusion that his victory was due to the assertive patriotism of the new ex-alien Americans, resentful of "the idea which is popular among the older Americans that they, the newcomers, are in some way inferior as patriots to their precursors." An outside observer cannot pretend to judge in such a question. But, for him, Mr. Thompson has a unique value as a flamboyant emblem of Americanism. His language alone is full of lessons for the thoughtful researcher. For wishing to convey that he was hostile to the enforcement of Prohibition by domiciliary visits, he exclaimed in the barely credible idiom that seems habitual with him on the platform: "I'll fire any cop who walks into a man's house without a warrant and fans the mattress for a pint flask." And again, "I'll break any cop I catch on the trail of a lonesome pint into a man's house or car." Another issue (of his own raising) involved denunciations of his predecessor's Superintendent of Schools for the introduction of pro-British text-books; and this indignant tribune of an outraged people, after calling that official "the stool-pigeon of King George," promised vociferously to "make the King of England keep his snoot out of America," promised indeed to "hand King George one on the snoot," should he forget himself so far as to intrude. For even Mayor Thompson's language has declared its independence of the King's English.

One would not cull these flowers out of pure lightheartedness. But Mr. Thompson's mind and utterance is too fine a specimen to overlook. One does not judge a garden by its rankest flower; neither does one omit it. Besides, his appeal, judging by the response, was popular. For he came first in the affections of this singularly impressive city by 83,072 votes. Should such a phenomenon be entirely omitted? The result, full of despair for what one commentator termed "the whither-are-we-drifting boys," is not entirely cheerless for the American future; since it seemed to indicate that the motley masses of Chicago are even now sufficiently American to react to a thoroughly American stimulus. And no less American was the response of his defeated rivals. I append, as a *document pour servir*, the rejoinder made by a great journal to the universal derision which the result excited outside Chicago. Printed as its first leading-article by the *Chicago Tribune*, it bore the slightly rueful heading:

AND SO'S YOUR OLD MAN

"If there was any part of Chicago that was not dominated by the bootleggers, thieves, thugs and dregs of the underworld," says the *Flathead Monitor* of Kalispell, Mont., "that section must now capitulate with the election." "Why this 'popular uprising' against good government?" asks the *New York Times*. "Shades of ancient Sodom and Gomorrah," says the *Astoria Budget* of Astoria, Ore., "of imperial Rome, of Paris when voluptuaries reigned! The Chicago of 1927 fades them all in wickedness and rottenness."

"Other cities," says the *Topeka Daily Capital*, "can be thankful they are not as the people of Chicago." "The whole campaign took on the semblance of a large group of thugs endeavouring to choose a leader," says the *Fargo, N.D., Forum*. "Not creditable to the intelligence of the Chicagoans," says the *Philadelphia Inquirer*. "Shows an undue prevalence of saps," says the *Wichita Beacon*. "Shames and disgraces the second largest city in the United States," says the *Lincoln, Neb., Star*. "An accurate reflection of the mind of a city which would sacrifice the interests of half the nation to keep its own tax rate down," says the *Detroit News*. "The spirit of lawlessness infects Chicago like a disease," says the *Vancouver Sun*. "Chicago seems to like it," says the *Baltimore Sun*. "Causes little surprise, but a good deal of regret outside that city," says the *New Orleans Times-Picayune*.

"Chicago's rum runners, bootleggers, blind pig-keepers, and the whole kit and bilin' of contrabandists from the whisky moguls and beer bandits to the alley barkeeps, make up a rather exclusive guild of the traffic," says the *Fort Wayne Journal*. "They have the run of the town if they do not actually run the town."

"And so's your old man," says the *Chicago Tribune*.

In the American family of cities and commonwealths, Chicago does not feel itself a stranger. It is at home. Occasionally it exchanges gunmen with New York or Boston or gets a safe blower from Omaha. It does not see much that is unfamiliar at home or elsewhere. It gets some hard eggs from the Minnesota and Wisconsin's woods, and some from down the Mississippi. It sends some out.

Its electorate is about the electorate of any other American city. Slice it down and it would make Cleveland, Philadelphia, Birmingham, San Francisco, San Antonio, or Boston. Slice it further and it would make Columbus, O., or Yellow Springs, Emporia, Kas., or Red Dog, Sioux City, or Painted Post, Plymouth, East St. Louis, Little Rock, Baltimore, or Salem.

We might put Honey Fitz and Sweet Adeline in the city hall, but it was Boston that did. New York turned down Mitchell for Hylan and Hylan for Singing Jimmie Walker, and continues to exist even with Singing Jimmie crashing the gate with his gang and taking the ringside seats for which the patient citizenship has paid its good money.

Indiana is proud because it has a governor in the penitentiary and Illinois hasn't. It also has Wiz Stephenson of the klan in there and has walled him in as tight as possible, fearing that he'll slip some information out which will make everybody uncomfortable. The Marion county grand jury has been discharged of duty in the klan investigation because the less any one learns of these matters the easier many citizens may sleep.

Philadelphia would count it a perfection of municipal reform if it could get anything but a stack of cinders to show what had been done on street paving within a measurable period of years after the assessments had all been paid.

We might elect Cole Blease to the United States senate, but we haven't. We merely elected Smith. We might have sent Hefling there, but again it was only Smith. We are not responsible for Tom Blanton in congress.

We have not elected Ma and Pa Ferguson, Pa first and then Ma after Pa had lost his citizenship because of the conduct of his office. That is a Texas contribution to the sanity of democracy. Maybe we've done no better or worse, but a citizen of Illinois and a citizen of Texas could shake hands in perfect understanding and sympathy. We weren't accountable for Magnus Johnson, the amiable eccentric of Minnesota. All we ever did for Ekhern, the former attorney-general of Wisconsin, was to give him desk room and some law practice.

We may have held our own with Tweed on one side and Sockless Jerry Simpson on the other, from their times down to the present, but for the most part it is about a piece off the same bolt of goods. This is the great American democracy, stepping high, wide, and handsome.

The pot and the kettle are playmates. Let's all get chummy again within the happy family.

That genial survey of local government throughout the Union may not be irrefutable; but it is not uninstructive. For the *Chicago Tribune* speaks, not for Mayor Thompson, but for Chicago, seated beside the dancing beauty of her lake and trying—sometimes a little truculently—to be an American city.

MASON AND DIXON LINE

MASON AND DIXON LINE

ONCE more, this is no treatise. Treatises abound. So why write another? Besides, a wise observer does not reach conclusions after three months of observation. His stay has been too long for that.

For he may dogmatise with freedom and precision on almost any subject in his first three days ashore. The first coloured men that he sees through a cab window on Washington Street, as he comes off the New York dock, will fill him with sage and final judgments; an evening under careful shepherding in Harlem completes his grasp of the whole problem; and after eight minutes' conversation with a Pullman porter he is prepared to solve it—with a few words to California on Japanese immigration thrown in by way of makeweight. But when the first fine flush has passed, he is less prodigal of his conclusions. Three months is just too long a sojourn for omniscience; since it teaches the traveller enough to see the outline of the problem, but not enough to solve it. Three days—or thirty years—is the right length of residence for persons ambitious to increase the sum of human wisdom on the Negro question. And then they get it wrong.

The judicious visitor will see it rather as the prime ingredient of American romance. If he is wise, indeed, he will welcome it in that picturesque capacity. For so many of his other expectations fail him. There are no buffaloes (except on nickels); palefaces walk around unscalped; and the red man has left his prairies to take refuge in museums or ill-fitting reach-me-downs. But though romance has faded with the wigwam and the thundering herd, Rastus remains—and Rastus (I name him affectionately, and without disrespect) is something. Romance, that most elusive Grail sought by all travellers, resides (I think) in a sense of being somewhere different from home. The citizen of Cedar Rapids, Ia., secures it at Palermo; Dodge Centre, Minn., may taste it in Madrid; and residents of Fort Wayne, Ind., might, I believe, experience the feeling anywhere. But it visits the Englishman in America most strongly when a soft-spoken, smiling presence reminds him a dozen times a day (or all day long, if he is in the train) that he is on a fresh continent, and that continent the home of *Uncle Tom*—and Harper's Ferry.

One traveller can still recover the authentic thrill of American romance from his first sight of the Kentucky shore lying in big, green folds beyond the Ohio, as a car spun him out of Cincinnati. Romance had not been noticeably present that day. For he had travelled hurriedly from Michigan overnight, dispensed the customary omniscience to reporters in a hotel bedroom, shaved, lunched, and lectured; and now, rescued by kindly hands, he was looking lazily out of the car windows and savouring the unaccustomed pleasure of fresh air. But there, beyond the rich curves of the river, lay Kentucky with the road to romance. He was half-way to Alabama; and as he stared across the Ohio, the eager traveller looked into Dixie.

I often feel that the American pen errs slightly in its treatment of Negro romance. The excited Muse of Mr. Vachell Lindsay insists that we shall see the big, black bulk of Africa behind the cotton-fields. His ear is always open for the throb of homicidal drums. Mine, I confess, prefers the banjo, since Afro-America has its own voice; and so long as half the white world is content (as it now seems to be) to lie under its spell, there is little need to analyse that haunting melody for problematic hints of a less pleasing atavism. I caught it once on a by-road in Texas. The night was rather dark, and a broad bar of light lay clear across the road from the half-open door of a little church. Someone proposed that we should go in and see the worship. But I know of no excuse for treating any congregation, however hospitable, as a raree-show. So we sat quiet in the car outside and listened, just beyond the belt of yellow light. There were a few stars in the night sky, and our ears were sharpened by the darkness. But there was little need to strain. For the small chapel rocked and rang with the gay reiteration. Pounding feet drove the lilt home, as the whole congregation swung to a single rhythm, proclaiming in exultant repetition that they were "*coming*, Lord, I'm coming; yes, I'm *coming*, Lord, I'm coming. For I'm *coming* . . ." They were clapping now; and the struck hands kept time to the lilting chorus and the drumming feet, except when an excited voice came in just ahead of the beat. That was the authentic note of the cotton belt. In another form it croons on saxophones, thuds intoxicatingly on the trap-drum, sets the whole modern world astir with the latest undulation of the dance, and then goes home to prance a domestic cake-walk. Need we pursue its ancestry up the dark forest paths, where the witch-dancers sway and the drums throb for sacrifice? Such research as Mr. Lindsay's would detect the Hun beneath the Hungarian and catch a distant gleam of Attila's wild riders in the *Rhapsodie Hongroise*. After all, Stonehenge was one of Dr. Johnson's antecedents; but no one has ever thought of searching *Rasselas* for signs of human sacrifice.

No less unfortunate, I feel, is the tendency manifested by one accomplished man of letters to treat the Negro as a fantastic tit-bit, as what Mr. Ezra Pound once denominated "a *specialité*," as, in fine, a species of literary *delicatessen*. Since I am no divine, I would not dare to question the theology of *Nigger Heaven*. But I prefer to view the Negro more broadly in his American surroundings. Dismissing his ancestry and his secret thoughts, I accept him gratefully as a romantic figure on the American scene. Browning once dated European romance from an age

When red and blue were indeed red and blue.

American romance must wear, for me, a darker colour.

So I was duly grateful, whenever a spectacled darkey with grey wool carried my baggage to a train. It was, I felt, the next best thing to an emotional encounter with a coal-black mammy. For me, the thrill was identical with that afforded to any American abroad by a glimpse of Tudor brick cushioned sedately on shaved lawns—that sudden, exquisite sense of butlers and ancestry. Each time the Pullman porter brushed me with his ineffectual brush, I too was favoured with a sense of butlers and ancestry—of faithful, coloured butlers and Virginian ancestry. It is a wonderful sensation: I know now why tourists troop to Haddon Hall. Besides, there was a solid reason for welcoming the association. For on a continent that rings, from Sandy Hook to Oakland, with vociferous professions of "service," the Pullman porter represents, so far as I know, the nearest approach to service in any European sense. He is not servile: but he somehow manages to serve. So does his colleague in the dining-car. Those iridescent smiles above white and blue tunics remain, for me, the brightest feature of American travel. Frankly alarmed by Japanese, I wither in the presence of Swedish chamber-maids and Croatian 'helps,' impregnably entrenched behind an unknown (and unknowable) language. Czech tailors paralyse my orders; and the Roumanian, who took my photograph at a 10 cent store in Kansas City, broke all his promises with impunity, since I dared not reproach him. But with the Pullman porter I am a man and—if he will permit the *cliché*—a brother. I can tell him what to do. True, he does not always do it. I know his faults. Did he not do his best to leave my baggage on a siding at Bakersfield and send me naked into the Mojave Desert? But I could, at least, explain the omission in language that he (and nearly all the bystanders) understood. For the Pullman porter is among the rare English-speaking elements that the explorer of the United States will encounter. The English-Speaking Union might, I think, do worse than give attention to his peculiar value for their work of drawing closer the two nations afflicted by that common (and rarely mastered) tongue; for there are moments when their nationals must feel extremely lonely in the United States. I am prepared to defend the Pullman porter against all comers. I know (nor do I underrate) his value to narrators of comic stories. Film-producers could hardly live without his exaggerated caution in face of non-existent dangers. But I affirm my perfect loyalty to him. Since all Pullman porters are called "George," Mayor Thompson of Chicago will suspect that, as a subject of King George, I owe it merely to his name.

I owe it rather to romance, to a deep gratitude that here, at last, on the whole shifting continent there is just one survival. He gratifies a European's sense (how sorely starved) of the past, as much as any Gothic ruin tickles a New World palate. Rastus remains. Indeed, I am not sure whether something of equal historic interest does not remain as well. For I have heard him under discussion north of the Ohio and far to the south, whilst an indescribable brown dog—a pointed dog, that was just dog and nothing more—tiptoed deliberately before our halted car across a deeply rutted road that ran between the decomposing wooden houses of George and Rastus and their cousins; and as the Southern talk ran on, I wondered vaguely, noting the difference in tone, whether the twin wraiths of Mr. Mason and Mr. Dixon did not sometimes haunt the midnight neighbourhood of their obliterated Line. But that fleeting doubt would seem to indicate a problem; and this is not a treatise.

EIGHTEENTH AMENDMENT

EIGHTEENTH AMENDMENT

THERE is one odd thing about Prohibition—and only one: it is no longer "news." Gangsters are "news"; "slush-funds" (the elegant term by which the less mentionable portion of the party-funds is known) are "news"; improper plays become, if raided, "news." But the Eighteenth Amendment is viewed with cold indifference by sub-editors and the many-headed *clientèle* for which they cater. Interviewers assail the arriving visitor for his impressions of the war-debts, Mr. Kellogg, divorce, the films, the President, and the Great American Novel. But the one topic on which they (and, in consequence, their interlocutor) are mute is Prohibition. It seemed a pity, because I had thought of something rather bright to say about it. But no one asked me. The American mind, it seemed, was made up on the subject. I never gathered quite distinctly in which direction it was made up. Perhaps in both; like those hotels which chain a corkscrew to the bathroom wall just underneath the notice requesting visitors to assist the management in its endeavours to enforce the law. Laodicean, if you will; but hospitable. You pay your money and you take your choice. Indeed, I am not sure whether that cryptic invitation does not embody the present attitude of the United States to the Eighteenth Amendment.

There is a good deal to be said for that arrest of judgment. For social experiments on such a scale can hardly be appraised within a generation or so of their initiation. It is a facile hallucination to credit Prohibition with the industrial prosperity of 1927, since booms have larger causes than slight adjustments in the habits of the working-class. Besides, if a slump comes in 1929, will that be due to Prohibition? I am not prepared to stake the future of a bold reform on such turns of the economic wheel. We shall know in thirty years if it has failed or not. Meanwhile, it would be just as well for all of us—Wet, Dry, or merely moist—to keep an open mind.

This Rhadamanthine impartiality is not always entirely easy to retain. No democrat (I use the term in its simpler European sense, and without reference to the "solid South") can be altogether happy under the apparent inequalities, which are a present feature of the system. For, without recourse to subterfuge and dubious negotiations with bell-boys or unnamed voices on the telephone, the stranger will (if he wants drink) get nearly all the drink he wants. Champagne appears upon the tables of the rich; the moderately well-to-do will always offer whisky; and cocktails will be served in almost every drawing-room, though they diminish steadily in power as he moves westward. But working-men must go without—or risk the poisonous decoctions of the "moonshiner." That, in a broad view, is a grave injustice, however beneficial to the working-man. It may be temporary; it may even, for all that I know, be inevitable. But while the enforcement of Prohibition remains unequal as between classes, it is not easy for the democrat to square his ardour for reform with the broad principles of social justice. "Prohibition for working-men" is not a rousing cry, though one can understand the attractions which it might hold for large employers. But something more universal must take its place, unless we are prepared for the anomaly of a privileged class with tolerated vices.

That class, indeed, is hardly benefiting by the reform. Its younger generation, which was to have grown up entirely innocent of the taste of alcohol and listened without sympathy or comprehension to the laments of its intemperate elders, appears to derive a certain social *cachet* from the possession of a hip-flask. This queer utensil even accompanies it to dances, where it is shared idyllically with partners or emptied with a nobler gesture into the common punch-bowl. (I once heard a host confess that he kept a waiter stationed by a dummy bowl expressly to receive these unsolicited contributions and with orders to pour the stuff away.) But these unhappy aberrations may be merely temporary. Time may bring other regulations for spirited young people to break—a law, for instance, against smoking cigarettes or writing *vers libre* or flying the Atlantic. They are, in any case, mere by-products of the main process of Prohibition; and that process will be watched with due attention until a final judgment can be passed—somewhere about 1960. Till then we must be satisfied with provisional comments and a few notes upon the by-products.

A second by-product seems graver, from the American stand-point, than the absorption of a slight excess of inferior gin by youths at parties. We often read, on the more sheltered side of the Atlantic, that the sense of public law is being undermined by systematic evasion. That evil consequence (if it be true) should not be underrated. One is inclined at first to view it in a slightly comic light, to ask how baby's sense of social discipline can really be impaired by hearing Father narrate with glee how he passed two Revenue officers in the Subway with three bottles of Scotch secreted in his suit-case. But the American significance of such a mood is graver. America is not merely trying to teach the children that Father must be obeyed. For America is herself a parent, with the most unruly, ill-assorted family of adopted children ever assembled on a single continent. From Syria, from Greece, the Balkans, Poland, Portugal, the Baltic States, and Sicily they come; and in their new home a distracted mother does her best to teach them to behave. That task is hardly rendered simpler, if the sanctity of American law is questioned daily by the practice of true-born Americans. How can the simple Slav learn to respect the laws of property, when he sees every fifth citizen busily engaged in breaking other (but no less solemnly enacted) laws? That is the obstacle which Prohibition, at its present stage, may possibly oppose to the wider and far more delicate process of converting America's vast alien intake into the units of a civilised community. Local knowledge alone can assess its gravity. But if it really appears that the essential process of Americanisation is retarded by the chartered illegalities that appear inseparable from the Prohibition system, then America may possibly conclude that the price paid for social betterment is too high.

One other by-product deserves a comment. If one thing strikes the passing student of American crime more than another, it is the immense and costly elaboration of its equipment. Bandits appear in silent, sumptuous automobiles, blow safes with apparatus almost equal in value to their booty, and depart under cover of armaments on a scale sufficient to excite the envy of a South American republic. Not theirs the waiting Ford, the imperfect jemmy, and the cheap Belgian revolver of their European *confrères*. For transatlantic crime tip-toes on balloon tyres and defends itself from interruption with machine-guns. (No American criminal, so far as I am aware, has yet mounted a 'heavy' or made off discreetly in a tank.) One wonders, in admiring awe, where this impressive apparatus comes from. And then a wandering doubt intrudes its head. The fantastic possibility suggests itself that these, perhaps, are further blessings poured from the cornucopia of Prohibition upon the criminal classes. You must remember that the drink-traffic is not yet abolished. It still exists. It has merely been transferred by law from its legitimate conductors to a criminal class, so that the profits previously earned by wine-merchants and brewers have been diverted to the bootlegger. The fund that once paid school-bills for the brewer's children is now shared out by rum-runners, bootleggers, their numerous (and well-armed) guardians, and the hostile parasites that prey upon them. The gunman and his friends are getting a good proportion of the profits earned (illegally, but earned right enough) by a great industry. I remember a taxi-driver in Kansas City, who expressed a deep regret that time did not avail for him to show me "the million-dollar homes of our lawyers, doctors, and bootleggers." So it almost seems that Prohibition may be operating as a continuous endowment of the criminal class.

But even that is a mere by-product, though one would scarcely underrate its gravity. The main product of Prohibition will be (if all goes well) the transformation of a people's habits. I share the ambition of its friends; I frankly admire the boldness of their effort; but who can minimise the incidental risks?

PLAYTIME IN IOWA

PLAYTIME IN IOWA

I hear thy liquid accents—Ioway.
SIX LONG HOURS IN LOS ANGELES.

WHEN the young gentlemen, who live in Paris and write novels about the Middle West, expatiate upon its gloom, I lift an eyebrow. Not too far, but just perceptibly. (The same emotion rises at comminations on their native city, delivered by young ladies who have made money writing magazine-stories about Chicago and gone to live in New York in order to write still better about Chicago.) Not that I doubt their observation. For they have noted everything from gas-fittings to filling-stations and the gritty texture of concrete side-walks in accordance with the best literary models. *Madame Bovary* herself could not have seen it all more clearly; and gloomy enough they seem to find it. Indeed, they do not seem to find Paris much more cheerful. For those trained observers a common gloom seems to unite Paris and Paris, Ind. So I have sometimes wondered whether each of us carries his own Middle West within himself.

My own, though city friends looked sad and a little sceptical when I announced my departure for Iowa, was obstinately cheerful. Did I not have a birthday in Cedar Rapids? But that, perhaps, was hardly a fair test, as I had brought it with me from Europe. Of course, the world contains cities more readily adapted to carnival. The music of the trains (*obbligato* for bells) may pall; and there is an undeniable monotony in the four intersecting streets that compose the shopping district. But what market-town could do much better? For sheep-dip is equally uninteresting in shop-windows of any age; no *devanture* is really thrilling to urban eyes, when filled with agricultural implements; and even a Tudor shop-front fails to enhance the charm of overshoes. A slightly older churchyard round an older church would hardly add to the amusements. Besides, had that been present, there could not have been three movies—separate and distinct, and with a change of programme twice a week. Neither would a soft-spoken darkey in a shoe-cleaning parlour have put, with perfect hospitality, a fresh record on his gramophone before attacking shoes alluvial with the rich mud of Iowa and, to this gay accompaniment, polished me back into society.

For me, the Middle West struck rather a note of determined gaiety—of such jollity, perhaps, as rasps the more delicate sensibilities of Mr. Sinclair Lewis, when his exhilarated characters bellow "Well, well, well, well . . ." and follow that benediction with a joke that is a little like a blow in the ribs. But what would you have? Plain-dwellers must keep cheerful somehow. The inhabitants of undulating countries can afford to let their spirits rise and fall, for the ground rises with them; a sunset behind a hill may raise them, or a wide prospect from a hill-top will restore their emotional tone. But on the level man is left to his own spiritual resources, and he must keep cheerful without such geographical aid. That, perhaps, is why Iowa, with its fifty thousand square miles of cultivated land, jars sometimes upon persons who, less certain of their cultivation, require to be assured that they are on the *rive gauche* before they venture on a smile.

At any rate, it failed to jar on me; and I recall with a quite unsophisticated glow the acre-wide dancing-floor of a State University, that was one glorious, slowly rotating jam of young engineers, duly equipped with young engineeresses and played into a semblance of dancing by the unwearied thump and blare of a student orchestra. Whether they learned much engineering, I could not enquire; although there was a good deal of highly technical speculation, with a wealth of "breaking-strains" and "angles of impact," on the security (or otherwise) of the musicians' gallery, in use for the first time that evening. But at least they learned to dance and smile and talk and choose engineeresses appropriate to their engineering futures. And what university can do much more (or even as much) for its *alumni?* They danced, where dancing was possible, on the big, lighted floor, or sat out together in a long gallery that hung above the freezing Iowa River. All round them, mile after mile of Iowa lay, opulently cultivable, in the darkness; and presently they would go out into it and make homes there, with their pleasant manners and the survivals (if anything survived) of their college learning. Such social training may be, perhaps, a modest function for a university. But then a farming State may be a slightly unheroic corner of the earth. It has its private heroisms, of course; but it may lack the higher flights and deeper depravities of less favoured regions. Yet that evening, as the band thumped and the young engineers went round, I was wholly unable to crave for a darker, more lurid scene: I could not find it in my heart to prefer Montmartre, as I should undeniably have done had I been born in Iowa. There was no echo in me of the hungry cry once uttered by William James amid "the blamelessness of Chautauqua" for "the flash of a pistol, a dagger or a devilish eye, anything to break the unlovely level of 10,000 good people—a crime, murder, rape, elopement, anything would do." But then I rather like good people. So each of us, perhaps, gets the Middle West that he deserves.

ERMINE AT DES MOINES

ERMINE AT DES MOINES

Tucket: enter the Prince, attended.

Old Play.

NO, HE was not strictly what could be described as an impressive figure. I met him face to face early one morning in a hotel lobby; and as he stood there, at the foot of the elevator, surrounded by respectful men in bowler-hats and looking into space with the jaded look of a road-weary camel, I was a little sorry for him. He looked a foot or so above my head; for he had all the unnecessary inches of his House, although he stooped a little. And he was really very tired, this Prince on tour and lecturing at large across the Middle West. What Furies drove him to it, I never ascertained. But he had learnt a lecture somehow; and now the despair of royal tutors dispensed it nightly to respectful hearers. His route and mine kept intersecting. I arrived in cities as the dust was settling after his triumphal progress or departed in the pleasing flutter occasioned by his entry; awed reporters asked for my opinions upon royal lecturers, and slightly ruffled by this august and (as it seemed to me) unfair competition, I once replied a little tartly that as his public rank supplied the main attraction, no doubt the proceeds of the royal exploits were duly credited to public funds in relief of taxpayers at home. But such malice was hardly chivalrous, since he was far more to be pitied. His lot was heavier than mine. For where I could slip into town at dawn and find a bath and morning papers, his arriving train was picketed by watchful Mayors. A line of handshakes on a freezing platform opened his day; countless shutters clicked as he stumbled sleepily towards a car that whirled him—to breakfast? No, for a comprehensive drive to view the city. For what Prince could live without such courtesies? Breakfast must wait. There was a line of boulevards, two pumping-stations, and an isolation hospital to be submitted for royal approval before anyone could think of breakfast. And then the Press, to say nothing of a loyal deputation of his own countrymen come, as good Ruritanians, to greet their Prince. No wonder that he drooped a little. For Western hospitality, going one better than Alphonse Daudet, had written a fresh and still more cruel chapter for *Les Rois en Exil*, as it devised new forms of entertainment for its dismal travesty of royalty.

There is something odd about these contacts of the Middle West with monarchy on tour. Sceptres are awkward things to pack; and who can say which is the proper corner of a Pullman to stow an orb? The air, when I was there, was still quivering with echoes of another royal visit, enhanced by queenly charm and even (in the windows of 10 cent stores) by queenly willingness to recommend a favoured hair-net with a regal profile and the bold royal signature itself. Excited fingers showed me the very room where Majesty had taken lunch; and I heard the tragic tale of a whole City Commission that had bought white kid gloves before the royal route was changed. Royalty, it seemed, was very affable on tour. Long habit stood it in good stead; a lifetime passed in royal approval of hospitals, reformatories, and women's institutes had glazed its eye to the correct degree of meaningless appreciation. It smiled and nodded at appropriate intervals, asked little sympathetic questions, and was quite uniformly gracious. Sometimes, indeed, it went still further, inviting fellow-countrymen located at safe distances to visit it at home. I found one happy loyalist, deep in the heart of Missouri, who had been the proud recipient of such an invitation and proposed to undertake the long journey home specially in order to renew the thrill of royal hand-shakes. Perhaps he started, though I tried to hint that things at home might be a little different. But if he did, I hope his expectations were fulfilled when he reached the Palace. No sentry, I trust, no chamberlain with formal notions intervened to disappoint him, when he explained that Majesty herself had asked him to drop in. For royalty is somehow less familiar at home than in Missouri. Even my dejected Prince succumbed to the gay infection, inviting wildly cheering Rotarians to call him by his first (and only) name and confessing shyly that life held no ambition for him beyond a modest desire to be known as a good fellow. Yet, for the European, there is something a shade distasteful in this easy familiarity of royalty on tour. Such condescensions, we feel, are not for us; we know that we shall never be invited to call it by its Christian name; its profile never commends a hair-net to our humbler use; and as the carriages go by, we have the slightly rueful certainty that we shall be kept discreetly in our places.

Not so the Middle West. I often wondered what that privileged region made of these caravans of conscientiously unbending royalty; and one evening at Des Moines I seemed to get my answer. My invariable Prince (our routes had crossed as usual, and we were both in town at the same moment) was to be entertained at some stupendous banquet, and a thoughtful friend offered to take me. More thoughtful still, he rescued me from the embarrassments of the speakers' table and let me dine among the cheerful company that radiated from it down the hall. The hall was decorated with the stars and stripes tastefully entwined with the Ruritanian colours; and an orchestra played slightly uneventful music, understood to be Ruritanian airs, although ex-Ruritanians (who abounded) looked singularly unmoved by these reminders of their childhood. My table was frankly irreverent. Some hero offered to collect the royal autograph, if anyone would bet against him. We bet him a dollar; then we bet him two; but when we rose to five, he gathered a handful of *menus* and marched off in an admiring silence, thrust them beneath the royal eye intent upon its dinner, and returned in triumph to collect his winnings. So everyone was happy—autograph collectors with the sign manual, Royal Highness with a feeling that he had been becomingly informal, and Des Moines with the glad certitude that it had been disrespectful and that it warmed the heart to have a royal Prince to be disrespectful to. That was, I felt, the key to these odd progresses of royalty through the Republic. Then the great moment came. A Governor, with rare restraint, proposed our guest in a one-sentence speech that alluded in each of its four relative clauses to "our great country"; and royalty, unfolding almost to its full height and a little dull-eyed, responded with a pitiful little exhortation to the Ruritanians present to be good Americans, as well as good Ruritanians. It was as poor a speech as most of us had hoped: kings, we reflected happily, are a poor spectacle. Then we trooped off to see him lecture. After the lecture, at that happy moment when humbler lecturers escape, he would shake hands with five hundred of his fellow-countrymen. Then he would catch a train and recommence at dawn in the next city.

I saw him once again. Reading the programme in a New York theatre, I came on a familiar profile. Perhaps the eye was more alert; but the outline was unmistakable. Besides, his name was printed underneath, with the wrong kind of coronet. There was the life-size portrait of a cigarette as well, together with a message from the Prince intimating that he had smoked its fellows and adding, in an idiom peculiar to tobacconists but rare in royal circles, that he had "found them to possess a very mild and agreeable aroma." Poor Ruritania.

SOUTHERN GENTLEMAN

SOUTHERN GENTLEMAN

IT WAS a growing town. It grew in both directions —outwards into the circumambient plain of Texas and upwards into a tall and deeply cherished sky-line. How fast it grew, I never really learned; because (to judge from my hotel) there appeared to be a pleasing local custom of doctoring the numbers of the floors. I mean, you were consigned to a destination on the ninth; but the elevator seemed to get there a trifle sooner than you had expected. So next time you watched the numbers, as they slipped downwards past the gate, and were rewarded by the delicious discovery that they started at the sixth. There is probably some sound and perfectly sufficient reason for the apparent eccentricity of this numerical system. But ignorant newcomers may be forgiven for being a little mystified; and one had sudden visions of a proud citizen, beguiled by the prevailing practice, exclaiming, "We stand to-day, sir, on the eighth floor. But if I am spared, I shall live to see this room on the fourteenth. Ours is a growing city. Yes, sir."

But let no hint of mine suggest a blot on that bright picture. For Texas was to leave its guest with gracious memories—of more friendly hands, I think, than in any State of the Union; of the blue-bonnets starred among the grass (with dreadful penalties for picking them) on Alamo Heights, and the little churches in the plain that whisper in faded Spanish from their mouldering baroque the last enchantments of the Eighteenth Century; of the notice-board in the hotel *patio* that bore the fabulous inscription, "To the alligator-pool"; of cow-boys squatting in the dust, like humped quotations from O. Henry, along the Nueces River; of a hot pinch of peppery Mexican *cuisine* taken with caution on a stone floor at San Antonio, and innumerable ways of serving barely credible vegetables that call up a big, sun-lit portico and a low, shady room where smiles and salads live in a grateful memory. These delights were as yet all untasted. But that morning, as became my first in Texas, the sky was blue; for that was where I met the spring coming up from Mexico (and as I had come from Kansas City, we were glad to meet). The town stood up like a young daughter of New York—tall, if a little slim—and the whole place was full of sunshine and cheerful companionship. One even enjoyed being reproved by a policeman for crossing the road before the signal for pedestrians, that emblem of civic progress. But most of all one could enjoy the sense of all the things that we were near to. The sun was comfortingly near in the blue sky; Mexico was only four hundred miles away; and the past, the fabulous and distant past of Mr. Lincoln and Jeff Davis, was very near indeed.

One feels sometimes that Northern piety has managed to remove that era to almost too great a distance. Its figures loom in the dim mist of a heroic age; the Union leaders have all the attributes (and some of the remoteness) of the Round Table; and there is a risk that piety on such a scale may even defeat itself. For worship often dims the significance of the object worshipped; and the world stands in some danger of losing a significant figure through this insistence on his historical apotheosis. If Mr. Lincoln is one with Pericles, he may come to signify as little. But in the South the war is nearer. There Gettysburg is still a living and angry memory, and one may discuss Pickett's advance and the delinquencies of General Sickles with more immediate interest than any Somme offensive. There is a rare attraction in living thus with a past age just round the corner. Belfast derives a similar exhilaration from its sense that the Battle of the Boyne was fought a year or so ago. But, to judge by Ulster, Robert Lee and Judah Benjamin are better company for any man's spiritual health than Dutch William.

Yet of all that Texas brought us near to—tamales, 'bad men' from Mexico, mesquite, Spanish missions—one contact was, for me, supreme. One wing that brushed us thrilled beyond all others. Did we not feel for an incomparable instant the delicious proximity of the Southern gentleman? We heard his authentic accent, as he spoke of shot-guns and the good name of his women-kind; and, like an impalpable visitant, we felt the brush of his susceptible honour. For honour filled the air—honour, that had impelled named persons only a few years back to shoot a neighbour just outside the bank and would, it seemed, excuse me if (delicious and terrifying thought) I shot my interlocutor. The honour that evokes these spirited deeds was not, I learned, the doer's. That, it appeared, was only defensible by normal means. But one imputation breathed against our women-kind would justify him, me, and everyone in the most desperate and lethal measures; and so susceptible were Texan juries to the same noble sentiments that we could take them with perfect impunity, since no Court would convict a really chivalrous assassin. The shooting at the bank, for instance. That was occasioned in the course of litigation by an incautious plea on someone's part, which implied a disrespect of someone else's womenfolk. It did, of course; because the plea alleged that one of them, judicious lady, had been guilty of exercising undue influence upon a suitable testator. What more natural than for her spirited relations to pursue the author of the charge to just outside the bank and shoot him with a shot-gun? For the shot-gun, on such occasions, is our chosen weapon. I had met shot-guns before; but they were the unworthy sawed-off shot-guns of the urban thug, or those which project from the windows of Cadillacs when driven fast by the Chicago police on night patrol. Here was a very different shot-gun—honour's blade itself, the lance of

Galahad, and Bayard's point. I was a shade alarmed, being unaccustomed to the proximity of such fabled objects. But happy women-kind, whose honour has such prompt defenders. No wonder that they make such perfect salads.

MEXICAN CABARET

MEXICAN CABARET

Près de la porte de Séville,
Chez mon ami Lillas Pastia,
J'irai danser la seguedille
Et boire du Manzanilla.

CARMEN.

IT OPENED on the note of Conrad. As I recall it, that spring day on the Rio Grande was a symphony in three contrasted movements. The opening was Conrad—muted violins, a thud of muffled drums and, far and thin, the horns of *Nostromo* ever so faintly calling. The next movement—*allegretto*—unmistakably was Sinclair Lewis, hoarse with saxophones and riddled with syncopation, the authentic utterance of a New World, of Gershwin, Henry Ford, and George F. Babbitt; and the last, the unforgettable *finale*, was the purest Kipling. But it opened, *adagio*, on the note of Conrad.

The night train for Mexico rolled endlessly across a never-ending plain towards the border, stopping to clank and hoot at a few unresponsive stations and roll on again. As day came, the sky paled. An outline on the roadside sharpened and was gone, as Texas in the shrill green of its sudden springtime flowed unendingly past the curtained windows. It was an unobservant train, or it must certainly have checked to see the little group that waited at a level crossing—a brown woman muffled in a black *mantilla* with a grave, preposterously hatted Mexican in the full solemnity of Sunday clothes and a small brown girl made browner still by the white glories of her First Communion, all waiting as the train clanked by.

So it rumbled towards Mexico under the rising day. Somewhere in front of it a station waited in the sun, where incurious men lounged at the corner of a little *plaza* or tilted their vast hats together in endless Sunday conference. A morning band defied the hour of breakfast with the pounding time and wailing minor of a tango. *Mantillas* on their way to church hurried past with ears averted; and the big, pointed hats went slipping round every corner and up every alley on the mysterious errands of a strange town. Below the *plaza*, where the roads drop suddenly towards the river, the sunlight fell full on the Rio Grande wandering, broad and blue, between two bright green banks towards the Gulf. A yellow bridge strode into Mexico; and at the end of it a strange tricolour hung limply above a shed, where small brown men made passes at official papers, and the glory of them all—the doorkeeper of Mexico—sat superb in the sunshine of the roadway, belted with cartridges, a miracle of ivory-butted private artillery on either hip.

Across the river the road climbed steeply in the sunshine; and a little town lay in the dust beside it, like its unnumbered dogs. It was a sad, Conradian little place, lit only by the smiles of negroes and the eyes of children. You could buy fresh gardenias from a black *bambino;* but you bought them in a dismal drinking-vault (there is no other industry along the border between Latin depravity and the Eighteenth Amendment.) And all around the mud houses lay peeling in the sunshine. Even the soldiers at the roofless fort on the hill, strange little heirs of Montezuma, lounged in their ill-fitting khaki and exhibited their Chinese profiles against a peeling wall of unroofed mud. Dogs pointed at incalculable garbage. Children played in pools. And, taller than ever, the pointed hats slipped by on their mysterious errands.

But the note of Conrad, too long sustained, seemed to break suddenly, as the symphony swept towards its second movement; and unmistakably the voice of Babbitt rose on the air beyond the river. Within the sheltering United States, two hundred yards from Mexico, there was an excellent hotel. A kindly clerk, some bell-boys, and an elevator marked it for civilisation's own; and from its countless dressing-tables on that sun-lit morning it carolled blithely in large type,

"HURRAH!

To-Morrow is Sunday"—it yipped—"that Wonderful Old Day of Rest." Then a more soothing note: "We are mighty glad to have you with us—May we try and help you start the day right. We will begin with the morning paper under your door. We will be delighted to serve you 'Breakfast in Bed' without service charge—like good friend wife or mother would do when we are all fettered out. Please feel at liberty to call the office if we can add further to your comfort. . . ." Thus Babbitt in the morning sunshine; while beyond the river Spain and the heirs of Montezuma lay in the shade of peeling walls.

Then the melody changed swiftly, and we were soon *en plein* Kipling. That authentic note rose full-throated where it was least expected. For one had not looked for echoes of the Diamond Jubilee along the Rio Grande. The little street, where the *cafés* elbowed each other with their flap-doors and scrawled invitations to the parched citizens of a righteous Republic, was no preparation for the full majesty of the last movement. The day's symphony ended with a magnificent surprise. A more modern note might seem to lurk about those trellised barnyards, which the proud citizens of Nuevo Laredo call *cabarets* because the stone floor is smooth with dancing and there are chairs and tables under the trellised shadows of the climbing plants. Indeed, a scar-faced bootlegger, straight out of a crook play, slipped in with lady-friend, took the traditional quick, furtive glance round that blameless quadrangle of sun and shadow, keeping his fist in a jacket pocket that was deliciously suggestive of a hidden gun. That was a whiff of *Broadway*, of high-jacking, automatics, and the last naughty elegance of 1927. We seemed so far from Kipling. But he came. He came four strong in a dusty automobile all the way from Austin, Texas; and soon he was hailing us, shifted us bodily with our two anæmic beers to his

Gargantuan table, where we were made acquainted, swapping businesses, birthplaces and ancestors. We were, of course we were, Saxon beyond belief—pure Dane from Yorkshire, Ulster Scot from Belfast, something from Manchester, and one Londoner. Our loyalties (thanks to King George III) were slightly diverse. But the Breed was there, expressed in various forms. We jeered at each other's countries, bantered the Debt, the neutral, and the appointed imbecility of our various governors. The Kipling note began to sound above the quick throb of fox-trots emitted by a shirt-sleeved band to four circling couples. But it rang clearest of all when we launched (Austin was speaking with a fine Texan eloquence) on a high-coloured, ramifying narrative of Mexican adventure. We sat and listened, elbows among the glasses; and the smallest of the company took careful note of all that passed. The Kipling circle was complete.

It was a rich *exposé* of a crowded evening, beginning in pure conviviality and ending—no one quite knew how—in the far from Dutch interior of a Mexican prison. The occasion was obscure—a Rabelaisian insult offered to a stranger Ford left unprotected in the *plaza* was the pretext. Shocked faces came and went in the darkness; angry voices rose; first Mexican police and then the Mexican army swarmed like hornets in the summer night; and the revellers were soon surrounded, pricked with bayonets, and driven, led, and prodded into gaol, to cling to their valuables with the clutch of drowning men and threaten nervous gaolers with loose bricks jerked neatly from the flooring (Belfast knew the trick). "I made a death-line," someone explained proudly. "'Cross that,'" I said, "'and you're dead,'" eliciting a piteous "*No intende*" from the turnkey, answered heroically by the brick-wielder in his Discobolus pose, "But I *do* intend." The night, it seemed, had ended with a general gaol-delivery and much signing of official papers understood to embody vows under solemn bond never to return to Mexican territory. But there we sat securely sipping beer, our backs to the dancing floor where beauty tripped to crooning saxophones across the chequered shadows.

The story told, we left in triumph, two passengers in front to bear the driver company and three large men behind, all happy and extremely vocal; and as our forewheels took the bridge to pass the Rio Grande, our last defiance floated on the wind in a challenge to outraged Mexico, as six at once we bawled the age-old watchword of Texan freedom, "Remember the Alamo." For opening on the note of Conrad, the day closed with brass, wood-wind, and full percussion on the authentic note of Kipling.

EXPATRIATE

EXPATRIATE

Speak roughly to your little boy,
And beat him when he sneezes:
He only does it to annoy,
Because he knows it teases.
THE DUCHESS'S SONG.

THE young man wrote it to annoy, I think. It was quite nicely written; but the whole composition seemed to hint at a pink tongue protruded from a cheeky face, an inky thumb seeking a nose in the eternal gesture of defiance. Whom he intended to annoy was not so clear. There were passages that seemed to point to some obscure vendetta against the Paris edition of the *New York Herald*. But these were merely incidental; and since he published it at home, I conclude that he wrote it with the praiseworthy intention of exasperating his countrymen at large.

It was a closely reasoned vindication, in four columns, of those American literary men who have incurred their country's displeasure by residence in Europe. He explained at length the reasons for his own emigration and its (to him) wholly satisfactory results. His European domicil, it seemed, involved no disloyalty; since (if I followed his argument) it gave him a better view of the American scene. That is quite possible: myopic persons are frequently assisted by increasing their distance from the object viewed. I hope it did a little for his vision of the European scene as well. For he once startled us by sending—more powerful than Fate in 1870—a character to "Metz with MacMahon." Or will he have to go back to America to get that right?

The old debate whether residence outside America involves apostasy will always rage; and a cautious neutral has no desire to stray between those eager firing-lines. The issue may be safely left to the ever-watchful guardians of the American soul and the expatriates themselves. Columbia must spank her own children, if she wants to. But I confess to a suppressed desire to help her. We have had exiles of our own, of course. Lord Byron left us; Shelley preferred a southern climate; Mr. and Mrs. Browning watched the traffic from Casa Guidi windows; and even Stevenson fled far into the Pacific. But, then, did they ever give themselves such airs about it? They were not half so irritating as these intolerable exiles of the Boul' Mich' for the plain reason that they were not nearly so pretentious. They just went abroad because they wanted to, without a hint that expatriation is a form of virtue or that the expatriate alone can get a comprehensive vision of his own country. Byron did not insist that Athens was the only place from which to get a view of London, nor Shelley that the qualities of George III became more visible from the Gulf of Spezzia; Browning never contended that the eternal verities were nearer to Florence than to Regent's Park;

and when did Stevenson maintain that the best view of Princes Street was from Samoa? They went because they liked it; had they liked it less, they would have stayed at home—and that was all about it.

Few spectacles are more distasteful than this self-constituted aristocracy of expatriates seated, finger on pulse, outside their *cafés*, measuring the progress of their own improvement. But I usurp Columbia's function of spanking her erring children. For I had not intended to pursue the main issue raised in this singularly complacent *apologia*. To tell the truth, another aspect of it caught and held my wandering attention. Somewhere upon that animated page my young friend defined his attitude to Europe, a continent which (as he brightly volunteered) "American money and American methods are saving." Full of a rising hope, I read on; and under my admiring gaze the expatriate soared to the loftiest empyrean where spread-eagles scream from Pole to Pole. His countrymen abroad—the very countrymen from whom he had taken refuge "to live, surrounded by people, by music, by good plays, by good pictures and the stimulation of intellectual companionship"—these drab reminders of his childhood inspired him to the strangest heights of eloquence. They were, it seems, "everywhere, like the Roman citizen, respected." Were they not "first cousins of the ancient Roman citizen and half-brothers of the English Milor of the day when Palmerston was forcing even such old foxes as Metternich to bow down before the power of

England"? Well, well, well, if they are really as good as that (and I have not denied it), it seems a pity for him not to live among them. For one would certainly have chosen to live in Rome under the Roman Empire.

Not so the young expatriate. He apparently prefers to admire his fellow-countrymen at a distance, and through his admiration of them to despise all other countries. France? "It is Standard Oil money which is saving Versailles and the Grand Trianon from ruin." Italy? "Rome is almost clean and if Mussolini succeeds in evading bullets long enough he will, in his energetic American way, perhaps make certain quarters smell less like a garbage can from which the lid has just been lifted." England, perhaps? Oh, no. For he knows the way to "feel sorry for England. It is the worst but also the most subtle of insults . . ." One might be justified, perhaps, in taking the slipper from Columbia's hand and continuing her offspring's education, whilst he is still careened. For the expatriate, it seems, puts out his tongue at hospitable strangers as well as at his mother.

But, worst of all, this student of the international problem rounds off the unpleasing exhibition with a shrill and ill-mannered denunciation of his greatest predecessor. "It was Henry James," he tells us, "himself so thoroughly of that era of snobs and expatriates . . ." and then the juvenile proceeds to correct that mellow vision of the interaction of Americans and Europe. *Daisy Miller*, it seems, is now completely out of date. She would be shingled, exquisitely dressed, and full of cocktails—"the confusion of European men who cannot fathom the manners of a demi-mondaine in the body of an Artemis." But when Italian noblemen pursue her hand and fortune, we learn that she will merely murmur: "Why, shall I marry that wop? He dances well but he's only a bum." One may be pardoned for preferring the psychology (no less than the idiom) of Henry James. For by an odd mischance I read that very morning in my paper:

NEW YORK HEIRESS TO BE RECEIVED BY POPE AFTER WEDDING

Rome, March 31.—(By Universal Service.)—Miss Anne Townsend, of Oyster Bay, N. Y., who will wed the Marquis Pellegrini Quarantotti at the chapel of the Noble Guard of the Vatican on April 28, will be received into the Church, April 17, by Mgr. Mann, the rector of Beda College of Rome, her instructor.

The religious ceremony will be performed by Mgr. Caccia Dominioni, after which the couple will be given a private audience and be blessed by his holiness, the pope.

So one wop was not so bum.

SERVIDOR

SERVIDOR

MINE be it, Muse, to praise the American (or should I have said "th' American"?) hotel. The theme is large; but as I know far more about it than most respectable, home-loving Americans, I am plainly the man. True, in a moment of exasperation I once divided American hotels into two classes—those in the hall of which the arrival of a railway-train would attract attention, and those where it would not. But that was hardly just. Someone would be pretty nearly sure to notice it almost anywhere.

The hall—I never really learned to call a hall the "lobby"—was the first object of my awe. It was so very large. Besides, marble in great quantities is always a little overpowering; and marble was the invariable setting of that scene. Crowds surged in all directions; for the hotel-lobby appears to perform for the modern city many of the functions of the market-place in ancient city-states. There are shops in it as well; and there the clerk behind his marble desk performs his daily miracle of reading your signature upside-down, as you write it on a little card, and then greeting you with ready courtesy by your own name. (I have known unobservant men, whom this performance left under the gratifying illusion that they were public characters, until they saw how it was done—I thought so once myself.) There also stern young ladies deprive you of your correspondence, until you satisfy them by your answers that you are veritably the bearer of your own name. One name, indeed, is hardly enough: you must get it all correct. For mail addressed to "Mr. Alfred . . ." will rarely be surrendered on a bare request for the postal matter of "Mr. A. . . ." One wondered how much criminal ingenuity in this country has been devoted to getting other people's letters; and it was comforting to recognise the impressive system that has been devised to foil it—for sometimes you can hardly get your own.

I loved the lobby, and I still recall it almost wistfully. What sylvan music can compare with the call of the bell-boy to his quarry? Besides, it is the home of an impenetrable mystery. Seated around in vast and richly gilded chairs were figures of which I never ascertained the true significance. From town to town, from State to State, they never varied. They were just the same in California as on the Atlantic seaboard. I saw them all across the continent, immovably enthroned and sitting invariably with their hats on. There was a place for them to leave their hats; but they never left them. I can see them now, posed inscrutably all round the lobby. They never read; they never moved. Perhaps they spoke to one another; but if they did, I feel sure that communication was effected by some inaudible form of lip-reading. I often watched them on their silent thrones, reflecting, with Mr. Masefield's *Sard Harker* in the silence of his Aztec temple, that "just in such a way should the thoughts of the gods pass to each other, without a movement of the lips." I never learned their inner thoughts. Perhaps they had none. But they remain for me, beyond the Mayas or the Serpent Mound, the unsolved riddle of the American continent.

No less mysterious, though in a more domestic key, is one other feature of American hotel-decoration. What scientist has ever explored the reason for hanging caged canaries in the dining-room? The practice varies in detail. Thus, Buffalo, N. Y., prefers them hung in window-arches, while Columbus, O., concentrates them in the middle of the room. But why birds at all? And why canaries? I often asked the question, but was never answered. One glimmer of a clue presents itself to the enquiring mind. The sight of caged canaries dimly recalled a lesson once learnt in British coalfields. For they have a practice there, after explosions, of sending a canary down the pit with the first rescue-party. The bird, it seems, is peculiarly susceptible to poisoned air, and its conduct often indicates the proximity of fatal gases. May one assume that hotel canaries perform a similar office in the dining-room? I always liked to think so, to see the waiters serving with a wary eye upon the cage. The canary droops: a waiter edges near the window. As it falls from the perch unconscious, he flings the window wide. Extravagant? Then I should like to see a rational explanation.

Upstairs the interest is slightly thinner. Yet it is from the upper regions that the American hotel derives its true character. For upstairs it grows impersonal. A dreadful solitude pervades it from the moment that you leave the cheerful society of the elevator. Here is no chambermaid to bear you company among her cans, no valet among someone else's trousers. For, by a system that is efficient but a shade unsociable, these services are centralised—your water in the plumbing of your taps and your valeting in a tailor's department somewhere out of sight. For that, and for all else, you have recourse to your room telephone. It will bring you meals, letters, newspapers, pressed clothes, and washing. That black orifice becomes your only peep-hole on the living world. No maid will bob in with hot water, no man with "Everything all right, sir?" You may not see a soul upstairs for days, except when a half-open door reveals a travelling salesman seated languidly among rows and rows of ladies' shoes. (To the unaccustomed eye there is always something a little odd in those discreet displays of samples ranged along the walls of hotel bedrooms; and I never quite recovered from coming suddenly on an array of hats for coloured ladies, who appeared to like their hats more coloured still.) But, apart from these diversions, you will see no signs of life except the bell-boys whom your telephone evokes (at a trifling charge) from the lower regions. Sometimes, indeed, you are denied the infrequent consolation of a human face by a device that seems to typify in a supreme degree the slightly inhuman tone of the American hotel. It bears the impressive (and not unromantic) name of "Servidor," and consists of a hollow space inside your bedroom door with entrances from either side. You hang a suit in it and telephone. Two minutes later something from the corridor bumps invisibly inside the Servidor, and your suit is gone. An hour later you hear another bump, and know that your garments have returned. I do not doubt its merits; but its fine austerity is somehow wasted on Europeans, who rather like to see a human face. Perhaps such promiscuity is outworn, and I only venture on a mild complaint with diffidence.

But no word of mine must hint at imperfections. For, Muse, I undertook to praise the American hotel, and I am perfectly prepared to. Where else upon the inhabited globe is washing done in half a day and all returned with your initials carefully inscribed in ink on silk pyjamas or attached with loving care to evening socks by little metal clips? Where else is writing-paper always present? What other telephone is half so quickly answered? Where, if not here, does a plain request for tea evoke the staggering interrogation, "Orange Pekoe, Formosa Oolong, or English Breakfast?" And in what other clime are corkscrews chained to the bathroom wall?

SALVATION AND SIX PER CENT

SALVATION AND SIX PER CENT

BUT I must not be unjust. It was only five per cent. There is no need to magnify, in spite of all temptations to alliterate.

It was one of those large American magazines with an exciting name and the portrait of an emphatic blonde on the outside. She was what, I believe, is called a speaking portrait. I was about fifteen yards from the bookstall when I saw her first; and from where I stood, I could hear her speaking quite distinctly. Since we are all human, I fell at once to the liquid appeal of her rather more than life-size eyes. That they were fitted throughout with silky, if slightly glutinous, eyelashes it is barely necessary to add. That she smiled is an understatement. That I bought her forthwith (together with the accompanying one hundred and twenty pages or so of printed matter) is almost too obvious to require announcement.

After a few moments of dazed contemplation, I turned the cover and looked inside. A mood of comfortable anticipation settled on me as I opened the magazine. I should find, I knew that I should find, those intimate details of the life of film-stars, which represent to me the highest form of contemporary fiction. I should see them at the swimming-pool, the steering-wheel, the bathing-beach, and all those other hyphenated places where we should all so much rather see them than on the screen. There would be revealing glimpses of their new thirteenth-century English manse (of cream stucco) in the Beverly Hills and of the sun-parlour recently erected under their personal supervision in the Hispano-Mauresque style. I should bask for an hour or so in the sunshine of their expansive personalities. For me they would unfold their deepest convictions on love and marriage, on table-decoration, and the latest openings in Mah-jongg.

It was going to be a glorious magazine, with a new feature on every page that would trail away undiscoverably into that trackless hinterland of advertisements which makes the back pages of an American periodical call so irresistibly to the explorer latent in every Englishman. And these jewels would all be set and framed in those sprightly, yet decorous, scenes of country-house life which are believed to induce the purchase of motor-cars or the more majestic setting in which the Queen of Rumania relieves the tedium of Court life (and, perhaps, her country's Budget) by assisting the sale of beauty specialties.

I began, as a true fancier should always begin, with the advertisements. And then I saw it. It caught my eye, in generous capitals running across an entire page:

BUY BROADWAY TEMPLE BONDS
AND LET GOD COME TO BROADWAY!

I read on. There was clearly nothing else to be done. It dropped to a large italic and exclaimed:

A 5 per Cent. Investment in Your Fellow-Man's Salvation.

Backed by Big Business and Banking Executives!

There was a picture of a large edifice faintly reminiscent of the Bush Building topped by Westminster Cathedral and backed by a sort of Aurora Borealis, which it appeared to be trying to wear as a halo. This edifice, I learned, was to contain:

A church auditorium seating 2,200, together with Sunday school rooms, gymnasium, swimming pool, social hall, and ever modern convenience for religious and community work; an apartment hotel in the tower over the church containing 644 rooms, public offices, cafeteria, dining-room, and everything necessary for a first-class apartment hotel, and the whole overlooking the Hudson River or Long Island Sound; apartments for housekeeping in the two wings, which will accommodate 500 people; stores on the Broadway front, which will be very desirable and therefore bring in a solid income.

That, without a word added or subtracted, is what it said. I paused for a few moments in simple reverence of the genius who, after two thousand years of ecclesiastical architecture, had solved the tantalising problem so long presented by the waste space inside the steeple. And as I bowed in silent awe before the easy brilliance which had inserted a cafeteria (to say nothing of 644 rooms) above the church, I asked a little bitterly why

Wren had not thought of anything like this . . . a cafeteria and twelve hundred rooms, the whole overlooking Ludgate-hill and the River Thames. What a tragedy of wasted opportunity.

Then, filled with morbid self-reproaches, I read on, where a gentleman had appended something in the nature of a lyrical prospectus. Possibly it was just a thought more exciting than those austere communications to which the chilly provisions of the Companies (Consolidation) Act have accustomed us. It began like this—and once more let me explain that I transcribe faithfully: "Broadway Temple is to be a combination of church and Skyscraper, religion and revenue, salvation and 5 per cent.—and the 5 per cent. is based on ethical Christian grounds." The happy promoter then plunged, with less satisfactory results, into the more awkward field of theology in an heroic endeavour to demonstrate that his faith always "spoke in terms of reward—He approved of the man who makes money in the parable of the ten talents, and he said the labourer is worthy of his hire—and by that token the investor is entitled to his income." One had an uneasy feeling that the material was growing a shade intractable. But there were all those stores on the eligible frontage to be brought somehow into the picture. Uneasy lies the church that wears a cafeteria.

Then returning with redoubled vigour from this uncomfortable excursion into theology, the prospectus restated its main theme with the full gusto of a sonata. The throbbing note ran through the whole and united it—church, frontages, cafeteria, and all—in a splendid, vibrant whole. "It is going to be a self-supporting, dividend-paying church—that's what captured the imagination and support of the great business men behind it—they liked the robust conception of a Church that is not a supplicant but a producer!—not only preaching that Christianity is consistent with Business, but demonstrating by its own example." The dithyrambic gentleman added, after a minor ecstasy of enumeration and measurements, that "when each room is lighted and the whole is topped by a revolving flaming cross 34 feet high, it will recall religion impressively to the six million people who can see it." I am sure I hope so.

One sometimes feels that we neglect the true wonders of the world we live in. Anxious, for once, to do my duty by a worthy object, I kept an observant eye for its recurrence; and in a later issue of same stupendous magazine, I was rewarded. For as an idle fancy strayed through its countless pages, a familiar voice exclaimed, in large capitals, from the top of a page:

RELIGION AND REVENUE
GLORIFIED BY A WONDERFUL IDEAL.

Followed a list of "some of the keenest and best-known business men in New York"; and I was back in the old fairyland. The picture, alas! was still the same. But the haloed skyscraper was now tersely described as "a Twentieth Century Cathedral, Church, Hotel, Stores, Apartment House; Self-supporting Community-serving"; and another dithyramb observed that it was, "in a sense, a gigantic symbol of the incontrovertible fact that Godliness can and should be continuous." It would, it seemed, be equally visible "on sunny days, or nights filled with the sinister menace of storm."

In a *crescendo* of eloquence the new evangelist soared to his peroration . . . "more than a revolutionary idea, more than a sound investment, more than an architectural wonder of the age; it represents a spiritual stepping-stone in man's climb upward." A happy postscript adds the welcome news that "John D. Rockefeller, Jr., has agreed to take the last $250,000 of the Bonds."

JUDICATURE

JUDICATURE

IT MAY be felt that, as this is not strictly an original composition, it has no place in these pages. But what am I to do? It came into my hands in a perfectly regular fashion, and I do not mean to let it go. The enquiries leading to this discovery were irreproachably conducted. As a matter of fact, I was reading the newspaper in bed—and there it was. As it was there, I saw it. If it had not been there, I suppose I should have missed it, and the world would have been (I think) the poorer. But there it was; and having seen it there, I resolved to pass on the information. I mean, I simply had to tell someone.

It is, I understand, the practice of all well-conducted *savants* to communicate scraps of significant information to their colleagues assembled in learned societies. These bodies subsequently print such communications in their Proceedings, which are eventually bound and decorate the tables in dentists' waiting-rooms. Perhaps I may be permitted to appear, for this one occasion, as a *savant* and to communicate my small discovery. It will, I think, be appreciated by waiting dental patients, if by no one else. But I only offer it as just a fragment, a *scintilla* of evidence, one tiny, brightly-coloured section of the whole noble mosaic of the United States.

You will find it on the map. It is a growing city in a pleasant situation. As it lies well to the north of the Ohio and east of the Mississippi, no part of its apparent oddity can be attributed to Western manners or to Southern retrogression. It was American soil when John Adams succeeded Washington and Mrs. Adams hung out her clothes to dry in the East Room of the new White House; and there has been no Frontier within miles of it for a hundred years. As its population was very nearly 100,000 a quarter of a century ago, you can scarcely term it a 'hick town.' Its industries are old-established; and its citizens take pardonable pride in several residential quarters pleasantly diversified by hills and trees, as well as by that delightful variety of domestic architecture which lends their greatest charm to American suburbs in eyes familiar with the depressing uniformity practised in Europe.

So there it stands, a dignified community with a strong civic sense and an admirable train-service. Perhaps it is its civic sense (or else a wise provision of the law) that compels it to print *in extenso* the minutes of its City Council—or, to adopt its own (and, for this purpose, the more proper) designation, the "Official Proceedings of the City Commission." This full and formal record is a welcome substitute for the garbled snatches of debate, with which British readers are more familiar when altercations between local Councilors wake the reporter; and it appears in the local newspaper, where it fills several columns, paid for (I trust) at advertising rates. I read it, because all official documents possess a morbid fascination for me. Their queer, rheumatic style has all the charm of early Gothic sculpture. It has something of the tortured grace of stiffly smiling effigies outside a French cathedral; the broad comedy of War Office English is worthy of Falstaff's countrymen; and I can hang for hours over those departmental stylists, who effect all their transitions by means of the exquisite expression, "Having regard to which . . ." But I digress. The official page was waiting, and I responded to its call. It opened well enough:

OFFICIAL PROCEEDINGS OF THE CITY COMMISSION
CITY OF . . .

Regular session, Monday evening, February 28th, 1927. Commission was called to order by His Honor, Mayor Swarthout.

Present—Coms. Baldwin, Gruenbauer, Karel, Kilstrom, Oltman, Swarthout, Sweet.

(The presence of Commissioner Baldwin gave me quite a sense of home.) Then someone moved that the minutes of the last meeting should be taken as read, and the deliberations opened. They opened under the slightly unpromising rubric of

PETITIONS AND COMMUNICATIONS

But the standard rose at once. For the very first communication was signed by a Justice of the Peace. Better still, it related to his salary; and, best of all, the greater part of it appeared to be in verse. I subjoin the document:

To the Honourable, the Mayor and City Commissioners of . . .

40129. Gentlemen: In accordance with the request of his honor, The Mayor, made at the last meeting of your honorable body, Feb. 24, 1927, I herewith submit the following as an expression of sentiments relative to the action of your honorable body *in re* salaries of the Justice of the Peace:

Appreciation

For the Mayor and City Commissioners of . . .

Kind words are sweeter than spring flowers in bloom,
And smiles will lighten up the darkest gloom;
Pleasant it is when some good end is won
To hear a friend say, "Boy, that was well done!"
But all the world is dressed in gayest hues,
The baby has a brand new pair of shoes,
Mother's dear face now wears a sweeter grin
Butcher and baker gladly "listen in,"
When these fond words bring joy of widest scope:
"Here is that raise in your pay envelope!"
Wishing your honors health, long life and happiness,
I remain,
Gratefully and sincerely yours,

. . . . . .

Justice of the Peace.

To this domestic rhapsody an official hand appended the somewhat chilly acknowledgment, "*Accepted and filed.*" I felt somehow that the judicial lyric deserved a warmer welcome.

That was my find; and, I confess, it left me gasping a little. Few jurists could, I think, repress a start at the slightly unusual spectacle of a police magistrate thanking a City Council for a rise in heroic couplets. Or even in prose. I did not exaggerate his status. A city Justice, I was well aware, was not a State judge, and still less a member of the Federal judiciary; illimitable distances separated him from the chilly eminence of the Supreme Court of the United States. And yet, on its little scale, his relation to the City Commission somehow seemed to typify the one great variation which the Fathers of the Constitution had introduced into the familiar machinery of British institutions. I knew (for Bryce had taught me) that thirty-eight States elect their judges. I knew, as well, that local Justices are frequently elected or, if not, appointed by an equally elected Mayor. But I had never realised so keenly the vague position of dependence occupied by the Bench in a Jeffersonian democracy. Indeed, I had always done my very best to stifle the facile conclusion, which rises so easily on European minds, that an elected Bench can scarcely handle crime with the unflinching hand that goes with a fixed tenure. But as I read the lyric in my morning paper, I began to think—about Montesquieu and the crime-wave and the wisdom of Democracy.

WAR DEBT

WAR DEBT

THERE is no need to be alarmed. This is not economics. If it is anything, it is a Social Note. But it is just worth recording.

I had expected many topics—Prohibition, the perversity of Mr. Sinclair Lewis, Shanghai, the Democratic nomination, and even Evolution. But there are two that any British visitor will find predominating in his hosts' conversation—the Prince of Wales and the Debt. Other matters are lightly touched on; but these two return with the fatal certainty of a recurring decimal. Their consuming interest in the first (though I was never able to respond with exclusive information) displayed a charming lack of prejudice. But the second always mystified me rather. Why was it always on the *tapis?* I had not thought about it much; I did not think about it then. It had not crossed the public mind at home for years—since, in fact, it ceased to be an open question. But British guests are everywhere expected to unmask whole batteries of views about it. This one, at any rate, failed ignominiously. He had no deep resentments to reveal, no readjustments to suggest. Indeed, one remembered feature of those conversations on the Debt has made him almost grateful for the settlement. For it evokes a shy and genuine affection for his own country in the most unexpected quarters. Yet even that may not be altogether good for us: for is not the most exasperating quality of Englishmen their perpetual certainty of having done the right thing?

LES AVEUGLES

LES AVEUGLES

I RECOLLECT it dimly as one of those preposterous masterpieces of the Nineties, that were the joy of parodists when I was a boy at school. You watched a dimly-lighted stage for hours, whilst unconvincing characters in draperies did partly comprehended things. They talked a little, too. But I recall a comforting conviction that it did not really matter whether you understood their goings-on or not, because it was all an allegory. (For an allegory released one in the Nineteenth Century from all comprehension, just like a complex in the Twentieth.) It was all an image of the life of man or the growth of plants or the habits of the wasp or something. And nearly all the characters, for some reason buried deep in the author's lumbering symbolism, were blind. They were led about, complaining a good deal; and though nothing was further from their creator's purpose, the whole effect was vaguely ludicrous. For that gifted man had managed to make even blindness funny: it was never, I think, more obvious that Providence intended all Flemings to be buffoons.

But I recall that faded scene, because it always seems to me an admirable image of the modern state. That, perhaps, is what the author meant, though I should hardly think so. For the Nineties were far too deeply interested in the problems of the individual to think about the state. Yet are they not all, our countries, a little like large, sightless persons led around by small (and more or less unsatisfactory) guides, by statesmen with ideas, by journalists with none, by soldiers with obsessions—and, above all, by school teachers? For the modern state is very largely what its school teachers make it. Prussia, for instance. Germany surprised the world at large in 1914; but it surprised nobody who knew what Prussian teachers had been up to for a generation past. The British working-class owes many of the gaps in its thinking to the slack-minded Socialism once prevalent among a class of our school teachers. I do not know how the Duce handles his schools; but the future of Fascismo will be determined far more by the teachers working on their adolescent material than by the visible proceedings of all the adults that ever sang romantic songs and wore black shirts. And where in the world is the school-teacher a more powerful agent than in the United States? For the school is the one factor that may weld that odd composite into a durable amalgam, or the one solvent (if you prefer the usual image) in the whole melting-pot. The teacher —and with the schools I include the universities— may manage to infuse some common quality into the offspring of Scot, Pole, Croat, Czech, Portuguese, and Irishman that will bind the States together. He may yet give them a common population in addition to their existing community of flag and institutions. And no one else can do it.

That is why I was always anxious to know more of American education. For the school teacher is the Chief Executive of the American future.

Here, as on other sides of American life, the European eye is strangely blinded by the odd travesty of itself which America has exported with so much vigour. Fiction and movies have taught us to regard American universities as fantastic establishments located on something enigmatically termed a "campus," where young men with large initials on their chests indulge in exercises of incredible violence to the accompaniment of still more incredible ululations. I soon learned a little better; though my first illusions seemed to derive some confirmation from a news item, which I once discovered with appropriate alarm in a Los Angeles newspaper:

YELL LEADERS WILL GATHER

Southland Rooting Chieftains Invited to Convention at U.S.C. To-morrow

High-school cheer leaders from 114 Southern California secondary schools have been invited to attend the annual Cheer Leaders' Convention at the University of Southern California to-morrow, when Burdette Henney, Trojan yell leader, will be in charge of an all-day program, beginning at 9 a.m. and ending at 10 p.m.

The handling of the rooting section, staging of stunts, coherent and systematic cheer leading, infusion of pep, effective yells and songs, good sportsmanship and the relation of the high-school rooting section to the college rooting section will be feature points of discussion and demonstration on the program.

That, one feels, is hardly a promising *milieu* in which to teach the young Slovene the elusive elements of Western civilisation. But it is not the sole, or even the main, ingredient of American college education. What is, a hurried traveller cannot easily define. The Eastern universities, of course, have international reputations and a far simpler problem; for they are merely engaged in the normal business of a university, in scholarship, research, and education, only slightly impeded by those enterprising benefactors of commercial tastes who insist upon endowing Chairs of Book-keeping by Double Entry—though even here one sometimes underrates the heavy handicap upon American scholarship. It is an easy fact for Englishmen to overlook that the main subject-matter of most forms of scholarship resides in Europe. We are so used to living with the Record Office just round the corner and the Paris *Archives* an afternoon away, that we can hardly imagine the embarrassments of American scholars, forced by geography to come three thousand miles in order to consult their sources. A Long Vacation spent in hasty note-taking is a poor substitute for the continuous facilities available to Europeans; but it is a rare tribute to devotion.

Yet research, pure scholarship, and Eastern universities are not the most significant features of American education. Its most exciting work, I feel, is being done a little further to the west. For the teacher's opportunity lies rather in those State Universities of hurried terms and crowded classes, which Western tax-payers maintain (slightly under protest) for the advantage of their children. What he is making of it, I know too little of the West and Middle West to judge. I think he sees his business rather as a matter of elementary civilisation than as one of scholarship—and who can say that he is wrong? Yet I feel that we could estimate his work a shade more fairly, if he did not insist on decorating it with the familiar nomenclature of other universities with widely different objects. It was a shock, I mean, to be presented to a Professor of Landscape Gardening. It was an almost equal jolt to read in the college journal of a small Middle-Western town that

> the members of the class in art history spent Tuesday afternoon in . . . where they visited the art exhibit of the work of American painters which is being shown in the city art gallery. The commercial value of the paintings ranged in price from $600 to $6,000.

That naïve announcement might tempt one to belittle their instructors, so long as one regarded the institution as a college in the familiar Eastern or European sense. But once envisage it as an industrious and devoted Secondary School, engaged in imparting the elements to an agricultural population, and you will realise its solid value. You may not even raise an eyebrow, when informed (in the same journal) that a *plébiscite* in the English Department brought out *Ben Hur* as the most popular book, with *Les Misérables*, *Tess*, *Jane Eyre*, and *The Covered Wagon* among the also-rans, while Dickens was voted the most popular author, winning from a field consisting of Lew Wallace, Victor Hugo, Thomas Hardy, and Zane Grey.

Two facts emerge—the devotion of the American scholar and the gallant effort of the State Universities. It is easy enough to ridicule college theses upon preposterous subjects or Chairs with absurdly lofty titles (I believe there is somewhere in the Union a Professor of Advanced Thought). But that is not the point. We may judge Eastern universities by European standards; and they will stand the test. But the absorbing business of American education lies in the elementary schools and, on the secondary grade, in State Universities. That is where the broth of the melting-pot swirls round; and there, perhaps, the brew will find its solvent, the blind men their leader.

SLEEPY HOLLOW

SLEEPY HOLLOW

ONE would have noticed it, I think, even without the inscription. For a large picture of the Taj Mahal is noticeable almost anywhere. But when it is rather more than a foot in width and runs clear across the entire page of a newspaper, it can scarcely be avoided. Besides, the letterpress had seen to that. "THE TAJ MAHAL," it cried in capitals that were almost audible, "COMES TO CHICAGO," adding in helpful parenthesis, "The World-Famed Mausoleum at Agra, India." A note in the top corner, among the minarets, supplied the further information that it was "The Most Glorious Structure of the Ages."

I was quite plainly in the presence of no ordinary announcement. So much, at least, was clear from the highly unusual accompaniment of some blank verse by Sir Edwin Arnold, which filled another quarter of the sky above the Taj. There were nineteen lines of it; and as my previous acquaintance with this gifted writer was lamentably imperfect, I read them all. A little sensual, it seemed to me. There was a passage about

> "the curves and shades
> Of the white breasts of her it celebrates,"

which, I feared, would not be permitted to come to Chicago with the rest of the building. But below this perilous excursion into the realm of letters we were on solid ground again. For a plain sentence stated in simple prose that "Here, on the 111th Street Highway this great Temple will stand, alone in its beauty and symmetry." A sudden fear shot through me. Had the Government of India, in some moment of unparalleled enterprise or inadvertence, really sold the Taj? After all, transactions of the kind were not unknown; and even governments may yield to temptation. But I was soon reassured. For underneath the pool, where a lady in fashionable clothes appeared to insist on photographing a water-lily in spite of her male companion's efforts to distract her attention in the direction of the Taj, there were two names. "Edgar A. Rossiter," I read, "Structural Engineer; Hugo Schmidt, Architect." A large italic added comfortingly, "*The Most Stirring Enterprise Ever Contemplated—The Duplication of a Wondrous Architectural Feat of Three Centuries Ago.*" So that was all.

The Briton in me breathed again. I wished the very best of luck to Mr. Schmidt and Mr. Rossiter in their heroic enterprise. The replica, it seemed was to be executed in "white granite, marble and reinforced concrete, with ornamental bronze gates and fixtures"; and considerable prominence was to be given to "the sacred flowers of the Orient, the Lotus and the Iris, and the modern rose" in the scheme of decoration. What could be more tasteful? My kindling fancy learned in a happy glow that "the leaves, buds and stems will be enamelled in their natural colours and will lend charm, beauty and warmth to the design of the structure." But a larger type summoned me to the centre of the page, where some unnamed stylist distilled his rhapsodies in language that deserves quotation. "Poets," he cried, "have paused in sheer ecstasy to describe its sublime charm." (This seemed a shade ungracious to Sir Edwin Arnold, who appeared capable of an extreme fluency on the subject.) "Artists have tried in vain to capture the perfect symmetry of its lines and angles"—hardly encouraging, I thought, for Messrs. Rossiter and Schmidt. "All who have gazed upon its amazing beauty have been lost in wonder. TAJ MAHAL!—the final resting-place of a great King and his Queen; the poetic expression in monumental structure of Divine Peace. And now, a lofty idea, long harbored, has been put into execution. To America—to Chicago—will be transported this dream of the East. . . . And before long will rise the Taj Mahal of the West with its inspiring dome and slender minarets." I am sure I hope so.

But I liked him best when he was practical. For this unknown poet, who might have written an epic of undertaking, could stoop his wing to detail that was positively domestic:

> "Five thousand crypts have been planned. Rooms for families will contain from 4 to 20, and crypts may be had as low as $250! Never before have crypts been offered so reasonably as here, where interments cost no more than outside burials.

"The receiving vault, now ready, will be used free of cost until the Mausoleum is completed. Space is being bought fast, and those interested are urged to lose no time in applying to us for full particulars."

I should think not, indeed. For who would miss a chance to secure, by prompt decease, a free spell in the receiving vault besides eternity in the Taj?

He was a really perfect host. A handy sketch-map showed that Sleepy Hollow Cemetery, where this miracle was to be erected (the commentator adding with slight malice that "there are no monuments to mar the scenery"), lay "with the great super-highways contemplated by the State and County . . . within an hour's ride of the entire County." But his consideration rose to its peak in the supreme announcement that "every modern appliance will be used, necessary to heat, ventilate and aerate the building, and many new features will be installed to assure safety and comfort." Which of us would not willingly be assured of a safe and comfortable Hereafter?

THE YOUNGER MARRIED SET

THE YOUNGER MARRIED SET

HE WAS reading a newspaper in the shade of an out-building. All round him, for three hundred miles in each direction, the endless distances of the Llano Estacado lay in the haze in which the Mission fathers found it, when they staked their trail across the Great American Desert with a faint line of little posts. Those patient Spaniards topped each finger-post with the hollow stare of a buffalo skull. For there were buffaloes in the land, when Don Francisco Coronado rode this way. But now it knew no other thunder than the morning train in which I rode securely, a sedentary Conquistador. We stopped for no apparent reason. Beyond the tracks the usual store adjoined the usual hotel. A check shirt came out to look at us and went in again; and the invariable road ran dustily across the plain from the way-station to some unnamed place below the horizon. There was one figure, though, reading a newspaper in the shade of an outbuilding. And this is what he read:

MARRIAGE OF LOCAL COUPLE IS SURPRISE

The announcement which has been made by Mr. and Mrs. H. E. Hertner, of the marriage of their granddaughter, Elizabeth

Spegal, to Dewey Morris, both of Amarillo, will come as a complete surprise to their many friends. Mr. and Mrs. Morris were married December 15, 1926, and for three months it has been kept a secret.

The bride is a graduate of St. Mary's Academy of 1925 and has grown to young womanhood in Amarillo. She is at present assisting Miss Grace Hamilton in her piano studies, where she is taking a music teacher's course under her.

The groom is the son of R. P. Morris, formerly of Amarillo. He is employed at the Central fire station, where he has held a responsible position for several years.

Mr. and Mrs. Morris are at home in their beautiful new home at 3504 South Polk Street. Both have a host of friends in the city who wish them well.

No stranger contrast awaits the enquiring European than this odd blend of Society intelligence with the Great Open Spaces. One had read before about a fireman's wedding. For firemen, as befits a race of heroes, are not wholly celibate even in Europe. Indeed, their nuptials form the subject of at least one rousing lyric, justly esteemed for public recitation. But in the Old World the theme was never treated with half so much social gusto.

Let it not be thought that the mood is one peculiar to Amarillo, Texas. For it prevails throughout the Union. The social columns of the morning papers pullulate with news of the Younger Married Set; an envious eye is filled with an illimitable vista of Society Matrons and their doings; nor is there any dearth of exclusive entertainments arranged by *débutantes*. Before whom they made their *début* or in what Drawing-room they dipped their ostrich feathers to what potentate, we may never learn. Nor can the European mind ever hope to fathom the social niceties of the more cryptic category of "sub-debs." (Small wonder that Henry James, resolved to paint a social scene, fled to the simpler classifications of the Old World.) But there they are. As one reads the Society page, a hierarchy of immense complication rises upon the astonished gaze; and the light that beats on Belgravia or the Faubourg seems to pale by comparison with the white blaze projected by transatlantic journalism upon its favoured few.

Are they, indeed, so few? To minds accustomed to the more restricted castes of Europe, their very numbers would appear to be quite the strangest feature of the whole exhibition. For in this freer air all men (or very nearly all) are "clubmen," and so many functions are graded as "exclusive" that one is left politely wondering who remains to be excluded. You recall the paragraph of the *Gopher Prairie Weekly Dauntless* in Mr. Sinclair Lewis' realistic fancy, which stated that the bride's family "are socially prominent in Minneapolis and Mankato." It is a baffling scene. If you like easy explanations, you may conclude that it is mainly due to a mere accident of terminology; that American journalism, I mean, has just imported its social vocabulary in bulk from Europe without particular regard to the meanings that it would bear when it arrived in the New World. For manifestly terms that are apt enough at Deauville may read a trifle differently when applied to Red Dog or Yuba Dam. That, however, is a rationalist's conclusion; and I dislike the uneventful argument of rationalists—it is always far too reasonable to be true. Besides, I prefer to see a deeper meaning in the immense social proliferation of the United States. Surely this universal prevalence of Society Hostesses indicates that the Republic has at last performed successfully its noble task of levelling. Its enemies (and some of its friends, as well) proclaimed that it would level down. But, as we see, their hopes are gloriously disappointed. For it has levelled up; and all society is now in Society.

The unpleasing modern would, of course, prefer a more tortuous explanation in his own nasty manner. He, I am perfectly convinced, would wish to see a demonstration of the questionable truths of psychoanalysis. Quoting the tragic instance of the maiden lady who . . . (but why particularise?), he will undoubtedly ask us to believe that something darker lies behind the innocent American taste for ranks and grades and hierarchies, for Klansmen and Knighthoods of Columbus. These, he explains, are the mere substitutes for something lost beyond recall and craved for without end, for the ranked society of squire and peer and bishop which the Fathers of the Republic put bravely behind them in their great experiment. Perhaps their sons are less austere and with the tendency (once so fatal to Lot's wife) of looking over their shoulders at regretted scenes. If so, we may recognise dream-duchesses in the Society Matrons and princes-that-might-have-been in the Younger Married Set.

I doubt it, though. Whole nations are unlikely to comply with Freudian psychology. Besides, how much more pleasant to believe that the guiding impulse in these eccentric verbal exploits is a sort of delicacy, a republican chivalry of labour which describes the fireman as "employed at the Central fire station, where he has held a responsible position for several years." This exquisite refinement rose, I think, to its greatest heights in the following announcement:

LADY BANK ROBBER, LOVELY PRISONER:
RELEASED SUNDAY

Sioux Falls, S. Dak., Apr. 1.—(AP)—Marian Meyers, 19, sentenced to 30 days in the state penitentiary here for attempting to rob a bank at Vermillion, has been such a model prisoner that she has earned five days off for good behaviour and will be released Sunday. Miss Meyers has not announced her plans after gaining her freedom.

What *grand seigneur*, flirting a handkerchief in the alleys of Versailles, could match the perfect chivalry of that last sentence? Matthew Arnold once shamed Victorian England by repeating as a sort of prose refrain one brutal sentence from a paragraph about a girl—"*Wragg is in custody.*" Might not one string a lyric picture of the United States upon the happier line, "*Miss Meyers has not announced her plans after gaining her freedom*"?

The President sits in the White House; the Supreme Court sits at Washington. *But Miss Meyers has not announced her plans after gaining her freedom.* Order and happiness smile upon the land from the Great Lakes to the Gulf of Mexico; peace reigns in fifty million homes; credit is steady, wheat abundant, cotton just short enough to support the market. *But Miss Meyers has not announced her plans . . .*

AMERICA IMPERATRIX

AMERICA IMPERATRIX

THE Narrows of the Hudson were still sliding past, as young men beset me with charming manners and the oddest choice of topics appropriate for interviews with a visiting historian. For they were gnawed with an unceasing passion for opinions on foreign affairs. Politely oblivious of the fact that fate had held me captive in mid-ocean for a week, sustained upon an unrewarding diet of wireless scraps, they seemed to ache like a thirsty land in summer for a downpour of definite statements on several international questions of the utmost delicacy. Why from me, I did not stop to ask. Any taxpayer, it seems, is good enough to expound the policy of his own Government —and, for the matter that, of any other—in the hearing of this eager public. But cautious enquiry elicited the facts, at least, on which I was desired to comment. Whilst I had hung like Mahomet's coffin between two continents in mid-Atlantic, two states, it seemed, had both done the identical thing. One in the Old World and the other in the New had each been sending armed protection for its threatened traders. The coincidence was odd. But there, as I learned the facts, it was. For as the troop-ships drove eastward from Southampton taking the Guards to Shanghai, the U.S. Marines were trickling into Nicaragua. There was a strange resemblance between their missions, between the sailing-orders of the delight of London nursemaids and those legendary Marines, upon whose gallant heads the United States have concentrated almost all their latent militarism.

But there was a difference between the cases. There was, I learned from the mouths of my polite informants, a whole world of difference. I had not noticed it. But they seemed quite clear on the point. For it was this way. As the British troopers slid down Southampton Water and nosed their way to Suez, they were propelled, it seemed, by all the crooked motives of the Old World. Kings chuckled, courtiers winked, and statesmen whispered evilly behind gnarled fingers at their going. It was (was it not?) a striking recrudescence of British imperialism—and what did I think about it? By way of answer I enquired politely for news of the U.S. Marines, those eager saviours of Central America from its baser instincts. As they slipped out of San Diego and turned towards Nicaragua, the sunshine (so I gathered) was on their foreheads. For they went about the blameless business of the New World. No sinister intent, no kings, no taint of selfishness; just business of the highest character, purely disinterested and quite legitimate—not even Big Business.

The contrast was instructive; and I did my best to profit by the lesson, to get the new perspective in the clear American light. A Guardsman ordered East to stand between a scared community and a resurgent

China was (probably) the minion of some dark imperialistic design. Did he not wear a crown—and even a unicorn—upon his buttons? But a Marine ordered South to stand in precisely the same attitude before a far less adequate enemy was, beyond all doubt and guessing, beyond even Mr. Wilson's cherished "peradventure," a missionary of something immaculate. For it was unthinkable that broad-browed Washington should take the taint, the Old World taint, of imperialism.

I heard; I bowed the head; but even in this respectful posture, a haze of irreverent doubt began to rise. Was there, I wondered, some insidious form in which the creeping virus of imperialism might perhaps have entered the young veins of a New World? Marines and neutral zones, the mildly reasoned Note, the monthly, weekly, daily admonition from the State Department, the treaty of perpetual friendship—were these the latest technique of imperialism? Had Mr. Kellogg found a new way to commit old sins? The uneasy questions rose unanswered, and I walked hastily ashore.

Imperialism is, after all, a shifting thing. Its form has varied from one century to the next and, still more widely, from one continent to the next. In its first simple form it grasped at universal domination. Rome and her imitators were the first European masters of the art. To reduce the habitable globe (or plane) to a single allegiance was the simple object of the first imperialists. One law, one Senate, and one coinage seemed to be the aims of universal empire, as it was practised by the more aggressive Cæsars. The picture was inspiring; and long after Rome had crumbled from empire into papacy, it inspired the Romanisers—Charlemagne and Augustus. That was the first and crudest form in which imperialism dawned on Europe. But even then there were wide variations between the practices of different continents. For while the Emperor hung Paris with captured flags, Jenghis Khan heaped a pile of heads before his door. Other continents, other manners. But within the limits of these regional variations, the aims of imperialism were identical—a single authority administering all the territory in sight. And in that ideal Napoleon was one with Nerva.

Europe, fragmented by the fall of Rome and still further atomised by the Reformation, was perpetually unfriendly to this simple design; and history became a long record of resistance to ambitious projects of universal domination. It was the function, preeminently, of Great Britain to focus this temper of national independence and anti-imperialism. The British Isles slipped at a comparatively early stage from the Roman grasp; they were an early centre of insurrection from Rome's successor, the universal Church; Spain's slow encirclement of Europe and even of the world, the large design which grasped Madrid, Vienna, Brussels, North Italy, and even the Americas, was challenged by the carronades of Elizabethan seamen and foundered in the deep Hebridean waters which engulfed the Great Armada; the French effort towards the same goal was foiled by Dutch William with a British army, and crumbled finally before Marlborough and the troopers who "swore terribly in Flanders" under Queen Anne; the bullrush of Napoleon was worn down by British seapower and took the final blow from the cool matador who waited on the ridge in front of the little village of Waterloo; and the latest aspirant to universal empire, the hair-brained practitioner of every art but that of government who passes his days at Doorn, owes much of his solitary leisure to the British effort, which expended men, ships, and money in four years of splendid prodigality.

Such, in the roughest outline, is the record of universal domination in the last fifteen centuries of Europe's history. Much has been omitted. But as the shadows of Hildebrand, of Charlemagne, of Charles V, of Louis XIV, of Napoleon flit unregarded by, one fact emerges; Europe instinctively resists a single domination. This phase of imperialism, apart from its almost involuntary recrudescence in the German dream of empire, was ended in the first quarters of the Nineteenth Century. But in the years that followed, it found a mild successor. Resigning hopes of universal domination over the closely inhabited areas covered by the European state-system, nations began to grasp at the easier prize of overseas dominion. In this phase Great Britain led—unconsciously, as is the way of British thought in matters of extreme importance. Through the years which followed the diminution of the first British Empire by the secession of its American Colonies, a second British Empire was rapidly assembled. Much remained of its predecessor—the Canadas, India, and a rich supply of sugar-islands. But in the years of European conflict, which determined the defeat of the French design of universal domination, British policy reached out beyond the visible horizons of Europe and made a second Empire. South Africa, Ceylon, advancing frontiers within India itself, East Indies, and unrecorded islands in every sea observed the steady march of British control.

The tendency was largely undiscovered by Europe, still interested in the checks and balances of its purely continental system. But it proceeded steadily in the years between Waterloo and 1870. Mainly unconscious, it resulted from the vague urge of population, of adventurous pioneers (for the Old World can show as many pioneer virtues as the New—is not the New World itself a monument to Old-World pioneering?), of judicious traders in pursuit of export markets, of mere patriotism exhibited by enterprising captains, who hoisted a flag and read a proclamation of annexation in a circle of respectful natives. The process was scarcely observed by other Powers, though France was stirred to emulation by a recollection of former colonial ardours and the convenient proximity of Algeria. It has been called, for want of a better name, imperialism; and it rests undoubtedly on the desire to build an empire and on a belief that the empire's law is best for all within its circle. But the ideal which prompted it is something very different from the crude ambitions of the Cæsars and their less fortunate imitators. For it partakes largely of the humbler aspirations of the exporting trader, of the desire of Manchester to clothe the heathen in a sufficiency of Manchester goods, of the doctor's and the missionary's faith in the superior virtues of his own civilisation. And there is this broad distinction to be made between the imperialism of Cecil Rhodes and that of Julius Cæsar, that it flowed mainly to the empty spaces of the earth; its goal was Bulawayo rather than the streets of Paris.

How far the world has gained or lost by a century of British expansion there is no need to appraise. The process of expansion is undoubted, and the beliefs behind it bear the simple collective title of imperialism. In its later stages the advance became a shade less confident. Where once the world had seen a bold series of annexations and frontiers had advanced quite unashamed, it began to observe the more diffident method of the Sphere of Influence, of suzerainty, of politely concealed Protectorates. No more the proclamation in the awed circle of natives, the flag fluttering on the tropic air, and the pounding salute. Now frontiers advance more delicately, a little in the manner of the lamented Agag. For imperialism was becoming less sure of itself, less certain of the blessings of good government and ordered commerce; and its tone became most apologetic.

I may be wrong. But in the latest devices of American policy I seem to detect a further shading of the bold imperialist design, a method of approach to the desired objective more delicate than Agag's. For methods vary with the march of time, and their variations are all in the direction of an increasing gentleness. The modern statesman annexes almost with a gesture of motherhood. His sterner predecessors, confronted with a prize, incontinently grabbed it—his grandfather by simple annexation, his father by a rigmarole about Spheres of Influence. But the softer tread of our contemporaries disdains such brutal footsteps. It advances under cover of a vigorous protestation of belief in the essential independence of the coveted object—and to lend it money. An occasional landing-party of Marines may keep a watchful eye on the security, but always with a stern insistence that it is no property of theirs. As the game develops, the object of desire may be impelled (with perfect freedom of action, but one eye on the Marines) to enter a treaty of perpetual friendship and dependence with and upon the absorbing Power. There will be no vulgar annexation. That is precisely where the method of Naboth's vineyard differs from that of Wall Street.

Is this delicate technique the latest variation in the Old-World theme of imperialism? I wonder, and am half inclined to think so. If so, I trust that the stern judges of the New World will be a trifle less severe upon the historical shortcomings of the Old. For they seem to be heirs to one, at least, of its vices in an attenuated form. Kid-glove imperialism is no more defensible on abstract principles of human justice than the full-blooded variety. Can we be sure that the United States, after a brief experiment in annexation, has not entered upon a more insidious form of concealed imperialism? Such outspoken critics must not complain if they occasionally attract a touch of comment from a politely interested world. For what is more delightful to the convicted sinner than to detect at least one mote in his critic's eye? And the Old World is left with a slightly irreverent wonder whether the purities of the Monroe Doctrine are not lightly dusted over with the faintest film of imperial ambition. If so, there is room for hope that its adherents will be less critical of similar ambition in others. Others, at any rate, rejoice to see the young man following in father's footsteps—and trust that in the future he will be a trifle less severe on father.

Such were the half-formed doubts that rose as reporters told a traveller the news from Nicaragua and China, and the big ship slid up the Narrows towards the tall, unlikely towers.

A PEAK IN DARIEN

A PEAK IN DARIEN

SILENCE, I understood, was customary on these occasions; and, as a well-read Conquistador who knew his business, I was duly silent. Most people would have been, after three days consisting mainly of hurrying nine miles from Los Angeles to Pasadena to keep appointments, nine miles back again to dress for dinner, and a last eighteen before bed-time, with dinner itself as a dimly remembered interlude somewhere along the road. To say nothing of occasional journeys along the Pilgrims' Way that leads to Hollywood; of a candle burnt at lunch-time before the shrine of Miss Gloria Swanson; of Mr. Fairbanks' all-embracing smile; of the "Blue Boy" looking a little greenish in his distant home; of the Sierra Madre carved on the sky, film-studios at work, and Californian hillsides ablaze with flowers.

This slightly flurried Odyssey left me a trifle breathless. Southern California, indeed, was almost too much for her admirer, since she had flung him, like an agitated shuttle, backwards and forwards across the lovely loom of hills and gardens that surround La Puebla de Nuestra Señora la Reina de los Angeles, which the heathen call Los Angeles, leaving visitors in some uncertainty as to whether the "g" is hard or soft. I was a little out of breath. So if silence was obligatory, I was quite willing to oblige. Stout Cortes could not have been more silent.

The morning train wandered uncertainly away from this hospitable maelstrom through an Italian landscape. Some genial lunacy had named a station "Chatsworth"; but the hills of Derbyshire were far indeed from that translucent sunshine, and there was a welcome absence of dukes. Instead, the tall sierras of the San Bernardino Range stared loftily above our heads, as we puffed slowly northward in their shadow. One looked up at them, reflecting with a mounting thrill that they could see something hidden from us. For as we wandered through the fields, the hills above were looking out to sea—to Hawaii, the Philippines, and China. So we sat on in an agreeable tension. Who could repress the very slightest quiver at a delicious sense of the Pacific waiting round the next corner? That, of course, is where one had a slight advantage over stout Cortes; for as he scaled his peak in Darien, Cortes was wholly unaware of what was coming. Not so his wise successors. No peaks for them, and no surprises; but a Pullman on the morning train to Santa Barbara. For posterity always travels in greater comfort. An exasperating man made despairing efforts to sell us sun-glasses; the retina, he said . . . But who wanted sun-glasses, with a prospect of the Pacific to look at? The train proceeded as uneventfully as though it had been bound for Brighton. Tickets were asked for; and one had an angry vision of obtuse conductors punching tickets for the Islands of the Blest. Small stations in the sunshine interposed wholly unnecessary delays. Deluded passengers got out—we saw them positively leave the train before they ever got a sight of the Pacific. More stations . . . further eloquence on the subject of sun-glasses . . . would the line, one began to wonder with Macbeth, stretch to the crack of doom? There were some trees along the track; and, a little tired of waiting, we looked at them instead. And suddenly, between the trees, it stepped into sight—the blue Pacific lying, broad and a little still, full in the morning sun.

I make no pretence of knowing what the first sight of Europe means to a traveller, since I saw it first out of a nursery window without memorable emotions. But the dim mass of Africa climbing up the sky beyond the edge of Spain is worth a journey for the sight of it. So are the big Atlantic rollers, where they come riding in to shore from Newfoundland and fill English ears with the last whisper of America. Echoes of richer quality sound in the pale Pacific surf—of Foochow and Samarang and Sourabaya; of thin Hawaiian music in the shade of Mauna Loa and gongs slowly beaten at Saigon; of unlikely airs fluted on pipes, the thud of drums behind Malay stockades and, faint and far, the voice of China. The little twinkling waves along those Californian beaches had once reflected ships in harbour at Manila or run through Macassar with the tide; strange towers in Chekiang had looked into them: and they had slept in the shade of sleeping trees beside the mouth of rivers in Borneo. For the Pacific is the road to romance, lying between the New World and the oldest.

But oceans are not there merely to be looked at: they should be swum in. Besides, unnatural foresight had provided us with the appropriate attire; had we not brought it all the way from England expressly to be dipped in the Pacific? It somehow seemed to twinkle less, as one approached across the sand; and was it quite so blue? The season was a trifle early, and a breeze swept the coast as briskly as an English beach. Then one recalled a little ruefully that stout Cortes had been less venturesome; for that judicious man remained, if recollection served, upon his peak in Darien. But Conquistadores must not hesitate. We plunged; and in the plunge we half expected to encounter sandalwood and myrrh and all the scents of the Spice Islands. Instead, we met something very like the English Channel, only a little colder. The long waves stole gently in to left and right; the green flanks of the Santa Ynez Mountains smiled down at them (and us) with a vague reminiscence of the Italian Riviera. (Even the landscape of Santa Barbara seemed as travelled and charming as its population.) But what was that in front? A vague hint of coast-line came through the sea haze. Had Asia come to meet us? But half-way across we turned back to California before we ever made our landing on the Chinese coast, to learn with mild regret that there are islands in the Santa Barbara Channel. So we had not seen Asia after all. But still, we had gone one better than stout Cortes: he never bathed in the Pacific.

GLAD TIDINGS

GLAD TIDINGS

IT WAS to be an evening of peculiar rejoicing at Angelus Temple. For Sister Aimée was restored to us after her absence in the East. The unholy whispered that New York had been a trifle less responsive than might have been expected. But her telegram from Dallas, Tex., bore triumphant witness:

Met at train in Dallas by singing throngs in white uniforms with welcome banners. Alfords and Fire chief officially welcoming. Building seating fifty-three hundred filled to-night with wonderful people . . .

And now she was to be at home once more, in her own Temple under the famous unsupported concrete dome, which Los Angeles believed to be the largest in the world. Small wonder that the front page of the *Four-square Crusader* carolled its welcome:

Together we have held the fort
And have done our very best
While you were away preaching,
Vacationing and having rest.

The last line, even with its extra foot, barely sufficed to give an adequate account of Sister Aimée's activities in the past fifteen months. Had she not lived in a splendid whirl of mysterious disappearances and litigation, crowned by the silencing of all (or nearly all) her envious rivals and a triumphal progress through the East? It was not surprising that Dallas had turned out to meet her train in white with welcome banners. But Los Angeles must do still better.

Did it, I wonder? There was something a shade dispirited in the crowd assembled under the concrete dome that evening. They were still trooping in off the Sunday streets, and the Temple band was playing *Poet and Peasant*. Perhaps that invariable overture of Suppe's is a little lacking in spiritual quality; or else there were too many sightseers present among the worshippers. The place was full enough. But new arrivals seemed to look about them a little strangely at the blue-gowned ushers, at the rousing banners round the gallery, and the big stage set for the illustrated sermon. The overture died down; and as the choir filed into seats above the stage, Suppe was succeeded by Delibes, Delibes by Gounod. We sat reading our copies of the *Foursquare Crusader* to the slightly secular strains of the "Soldiers' Chorus." It was a businesslike periodical, full of brisk evangelical announcements, reports of healing, and statistics of anointed handkerchiefs "carefully taken care of by Sister Helen Bopst" and returned by the Prayer Department after being "prayed over by Mother Kennedy, assisted by the visiting pastors from the Branch churches, Brother Arthur and the Elders of Angelus Temple." There was a serial entitled *Out of the Jaws of Hell, being the Life Story of Mary Elizabeth Sullivan, formerly known as the "Queen of the Dope Ring," now proudly rejoicing as a "Daughter of the King,"* which opened with a singularly alluring synopsis:

> "Raised in a home where the teachings of Ingersoll had supplanted the Bible, married in her teens to a drunkard, Mary Elizabeth was shot and frightfully wounded by her husband, who then committed suicide. After spending two years in hospitals she was reunited with her mother and her baby son, only to discover that while under surgical treatment opiates had turned her into an incurable dope addict. Trying cure after cure without success, she finally succumbs to her apparent fate; takes up life on a houseboat and becomes a 'fence' for a group of gangsters."

This powerful warning against matrimony, surgery, or life on houseboats was plainly deserving of attention. In the current instalment the heroine (who carried a sawed-off shot-gun and seemed to keep a pair of bulldogs) was discovered smoking opium on deck after "acting upon a hunch, she did not want to have any stolen property aboard that night" and dropping her booty overboard, "carefully marking the spot with a broken twig."

But these feverish delights were interrupted by the arrival of Sister Aimée. She had entered unobtrusively and now, a pleasant-looking lady with a good deal of carefully arranged fair hair, was sitting in a big chair on the stage. She clasped a Bible and was draped in a long dark-blue cloak. A telephone stood at her elbow, and the waiting microphone of Radio K.F.S.G. was just in front. An alarming backcloth depicted greenish fiends in flight from angels with trumpets; and the space between it and her chair was almost filled with three life-size crosses. No effigies hung on them; but the construction gang (whose achievements were celebrated in the *Foursquare Crusader*) had gratified their sense of realism by driving three enormous nails into the middle cross and decorating their vicinity with liberal splashes of red paint.

Against this slightly garish background Sister Aimée read a short passage of Scripture, led the Temple in a hymn with a good deal of practised brightness and sat waiting, a demure figure in dark blue, while the musical programme drew slowly to its end. A lady played the xylophone; a baritone rendered some sacred music; and once, when a quartette was singing, she turned the microphone away—a shade uncharitably, I thought. Then she rose to preach and continued for about an hour. The earlier portions of the sermon, which were carefully composed and had reference to the scene set on the stage, seemed slightly strange to her; some awkward words in it, that she appeared to encounter for the first time, gave her a little trouble. But the illustrated sermon had its unerring accompaniment. For, guided by insight or by lighting-cues, the electrician followed her argument from point to point about the stage. The sympathetic magic of lime-light lent its aid; and as the preacher alluded to each item of the scene behind her, it was illuminated in appropriate colours. Her closing passages were more revivalist; her arms went up; and as they rose above her head, the big blue cloak parted to reveal a trim figure in white. The gathering was invited to participate, to join in concerted ejaculations, to raise hands for this or that. When the response was poor (and hands went up a little sparsely in the two big galleries), she gave delighted thanks for numbers wildly in excess of reality. There was a final call to the platform, a stampede of eager ushers down the gangways ready to shepherd penitents up to the stage. Coat-sleeves were plucked; neighbours became officious. But they mounted slowly; and we left them kneeling on the stage before the routed fiends, real figures in black coats among the scenery, while Sister Aimée smiled her brilliant smile above the bowed shoulders.

POOR LITTLE RICH BOY

POOR LITTLE RICH BOY

IT WAS a thrill, of course, when the big front door swung slowly open and disclosed a profile that one had known since childhood. Not that we knew the butler. For the butlers of the American great, though invariably British, are so episcopal as to be known to few except the other members of the Athenæum. We did not even know our host. But then one never did. Hospitality, in a charming and altogether novel fashion, preceded friendship in the New World. You presented "letters"; doors flew open; and you dined with total strangers—but you said good-night to friends. That day we did not know our host from Adam, though we had gathered from the drive that, like Adam, he appeared to live in Eden. Yet as the big front door swung open, it disclosed a face that one had known for years. She sat her throne, as proud as ever; and as she took the pose, Sir Joshua's drapery billowed round her. For on the afternoon we made a call in Pasadena, our respects were paid to Sarah Siddons.

Our host (alas, a host no longer) presented us; and presences no less familiar smiled down from other walls —some in Mr. Romney's favourite satin, some in the big, drooping hats that Gainsborough loved to paint. They seemed to wait for us in the still walks of English gardens, leaning lightly against urns; and as we sipped our tea and talked about the train-service, we longed to tell them all the news—that London was still London, although the Mall was sadly changed and they would look in vain along Piccadilly for Devonshire House; that no one now played ombre, and mantua-makers preferred a meagre mode; that poor Lord North had got his way and lost the American Colonies in spite of all that Mr. Burke could say; that Charles Fox had died a minister and the Prince of Wales married a German princess after all; that Samuel Johnson was remembered; that the town stretched far into the fields past Tyburn; that Mr. Walpole finished Strawberry Hill and succeeded to the title; and that the sentries still wore scarlet at St. James's. How they must ache for news from home, those elegant exiles from the Eighteenth Century imprisoned in their frames beyond the Rocky Mountains.

Yet their regrets were not apparent. They smiled so bravely in the Californian light. One might almost think that they had caught no whisper of the outcry occasioned by their emigration. For as each of them left home, the English streets were loud with lamentation. Ardent patriots, who had never bothered to leave cards on them when they had the chance, accused them roundly of deserting England. But had they? They had left it, of course; but mere departure is not always quite the same thing as desertion. May one not fancy that the English name is served by such ambassadors abroad? Greece, after all, is honoured in the

Elgin Marbles; so why not England in her exiled Gainsboroughs? That, at any rate, is how they seem to carry it off; and as the rosy gentlemen smiled at their satin ladies, the distant gallery became a sort of embassy, a piece of England.

Indeed, if there is anything a little wistful, one seems to see it in their custodians. For somehow the collector is himself collected; wishing to possess these figures of the English past, he is possessed by them. Those high-coloured ladies have had so many servants in their time that their latest owner seems to be just one servant more. For while they endure unchanging, they change their servants just as they always used to. That is the fancy that grew strongly upon one, as a gracious owner exposed his treasures. The pointing figure on the floor, that secured a few years of pride from living in their household, seemed so ephemeral. But the bright smiles upon the canvas, these endured. One could feel almost sorry for the connoisseur. He makes his acquisition, scores his little triumph, and flits by. Shadows we are, as Mr. Burke informed the Bristol electors; but are they always shadows that we pursue? For though the connoisseur may pass, the tall gentlemen in knee-breeches converse for ever across the gallery with the rouged ladies, the little children smile their elfish smiles, and Siddons sits on superb.

THE MAD CATHEDRAL

THE MAD CATHEDRAL

THE nave was quite sublime. Dim vistas on each side hinted at transepts; and one of the roofs that Piranesi drew towered into the darkness, though possibly the hand of Mr. Joseph Pennell had added some of the cords and scaffoldings that hung from it. Outside the sun was shining; and one had a sense of passers-by hurrying across a Parvis in the shadow of a big West Door. For here, beyond all doubt, was a cathedral. We had not noticed one in Hollywood. But faint music hung about its aisles; busy worshippers trotted towards side-chapels; and one turned at every moment to catch the glow of a great rose-window. A woman drifted by with her hair loose about her shoulders. It seemed a little odd. And then the chapels were so queer. There were no altars; and in one of them a young man in evening dress with a pink shirt-front and a fez was whispering inaudibly, with a look of nameless evil, to a draped figure on a divan. His lips kept moving, but there was no sound; perhaps the music drowned it. It was a queer cathedral, where men in shirt-sleeves perched in the chancel, directing cruel lights upon a silent choir dressed in the oddest clothes, while precentors in eye-shades stooped above their missals. There were deserted chapels filled with forgotten architecture, with palace gates, with Mexican hillsides, with cottage interiors; and electric cables lay about the floor like sleeping snakes. Yet in that noble nave one could never quite escape the sense of a cathedral. A shrill bell might sound at any moment and release a mad Jubilee procession of cowboys, cardinals, veiled ladies, negroes, Zouaves, and electricians. For the great film-studio resembled nothing more than a cathedral that had lost its senses.

We had lunched at ease in the Bishop's Palace. A smile of international fame had received us at the turnstile, and we walked proudly in to lunch behind *The Black Pirate.* Nothing remains of that festivity except a gay, remembered whirl of conversation, lacquer, salads, and the tiny sculptured figure of Miss Gloria Swanson, carved like her own jade. Still reeling, we had crossed a sunlit path and entered the cathedral, made free of its wonders for the afternoon. We sat about on camp chairs that bore the names of "stars," and talked—yes, positively talked—to movie-actors. All round us, glued to their megaphones, sat film-directors, breeched, booted, and almost spurred. I had never understood why those dynamic men find it essential to adopt so equestrian a uniform; and even now my uncertainty remains. Perhaps, the last romantics of the New World, they are still waiting, hopeful in spite of everything, for an Indian raid, prepared to leap on horseback and dash off, like Mr. Leacock's hero, in all directions.

Other mysteries greeted our reverent and delighted

gaze. For hours, it seemed, a dishevelled lady in an Eastern tale, walked down a passage, stared from an upper window, started in horror, and disappeared again. She did it beautifully each time; but if she did it once, I suppose she did it thirty times, whilst an insatiable director searched in vain for some hidden standard of perfection. And each time that she did it, music struck up and she proceeded to the opening bars of the "Chanson Indoue" from *Sadko*, promptly checked the very moment that she left her window. She might, of course, be helped by Rimsky-Korsakov to realise an oriental *mise-en-scène*. But what purpose was served by such endless repetition I never fathomed, except perhaps to impress performers with a sense of infinite directorial fastidiousness. Had I not already seen a small boy with a carefully blacked eye returning home *ad nauseam* to a humble cottage, where his mother smoothed his hair and bravely bore this intimation that their presence in the village was not wholly welcome? Each time the door swung open; each time she looked up from her knitting; and each time she folded him in an embrace of infinite understanding. Even an eager layman, gloating over the richly alluring mystery of the movies, cannot endure such *longueurs* for ever; and how the movie-actor bears the intolerable tedium, I cannot conceive. Before Hollywood received me, I had thought of him (and her) as quite the gayest figure of the modern world; but I recall them now as Trappists, vowed to a wholly ascetic life of unbearable monotony.

But as the lady started for the eighteenth time at her upper window, our monotony was generously relieved. For we had company enough. Effendis drifted up for news of home; Pashas of evil aspect accepted nervously-proffered cigarettes; sergeants of Turcos explained that Hollywood, though dull, was better than Newport, Mon.; and we discovered the hidden secret of the movies, that the great American industry is filled to overflowing with cheerful Englishmen. So we sat talking, with the lights searing our eyes and directors bawling "Camera" down megaphones, while Rimsky-Korsakov spasmodically evoked the Orient under the noble spring of the big room, that irresistibly recalled a mad cathedral.

FANTASIA ON A HOPI DANCER

FANTASIA ON A HOPI DANCER

MY HOSTESS'S eye swerved for an instant; and, that guardian orb averted, the determined man descended on me like a stooping falcon. We were all talking harmlessly enough after a charming dinner. But he had been waiting all the evening, quite intolerably full of politics; and now his moment, like von Moltke's at Sadowa, had arrived. (I record him merely as an isolated episode, as the one untypical American who very nearly turned me for ten minutes into that rarest of all portents, the typical Englishman—a friend of his, I subsequently learned, had just been elected Mayor of Chicago on the strength of possessing the same peculiar qualities.) Not his the mild enquiry on the dole or Mr. Lloyd George's war-chest or the private life of Mr. Gladstone, which had been the friendly staples of American conversation upon English topics. He went for larger game. For, calling all history to be his witness with one sweeping gesture, he asked me what they (meaning his countrymen) had got out of the War. The shattering question came at me out of a blue of gentle after-dinner talk. As I did not know the answer, I made none; but avoiding his accusing eye,

I struggled faintly to return to the harmless interchange of hotel experiences and sleeping-car adventure, which are the current coin of international friendship. (I imagine that Foreign Ministers link nations at Geneva by swapping tales of Pullman porters.) But my tormentor, strong in the justice of his cause, persisted. I felt that, wasted in this social *milieu*, he would have found his level in the Senate. Perhaps he has by now gone to his long account under the iron dome at Washington. He taxed me with a British Empire bloated, it seemed, with its war-profits, gorged with vast mandated territories, with the deep argosies of Palestine, to say nothing of the Bismarck Archipelago, that Eldorado of the South Pacific. I saw my hostess looking a little anxious, signalled reassurance, and parried gently. But in me, politely huddled in one corner of a sofa, he seemed to see all tyrannies embodied—King George's Hessians, the bloody hand of Cromwell, rack and stake, the fires of Smithfield, and General Maxwell's firing-parties. At intervals he remembered India with a rich particularity. I suppose I should have answered. But if there is one quality that I dislike in guests, it is historical repartee. Besides, eloquence is so narcotic; and I believe I dozed. The rich catalogue proceeded; but, for me, the listening circle faded . . .

Another took its place. That was a circle too; but this time it was a standing circle, ranged under a tall sky to watch something at its centre. I suppose I must have seen it somewhere, and his refrain had somehow charmed it back again. He mentioned Indians, I think. The circle stood and watched; behind them a mad landscape lay in a still convulsion, where an Arizona sunset looked over the rim of the Grand Canyon and turned cold. The ring stood staring towards its centre, where a drum thudded with a queer, arrested beat; and I craned to see as well. The drummer sat behind his drum, backed by two standing women. A pair of bare-headed dancers jigged at a sort of dog-trot, and alongside of them two dismal travesties of braves in war-paint—shield, tomahawk, and eagle-feathers—crouched and pranced with dispirited ululations. They pranced so dutifully in the fading daylight. Then the prancing checked for a moment, and the feathered chief (for surely the enterprising railway company must have supplied us with a chief) announced without emotion that the next dance would be a prayer for rain—"for rain that is very necessary to our stock-raising and agriculture, *and rain is very scarce on our Reservation.*" He spoke without the faintest bitterness, and the watching circle scarcely seemed to listen. Then the drum was thudding once again, and the dull eyes came round in the wooden faces . . . "*very scarce on our Reservation.*" It was colder now, and an evening chill began to steal up out of the Canyon. The drumming died away; a coin or so fell into the ring; and the circle melted. For we had a train to catch, the Rockies and the Great Plains to traverse, a whole continent to cross . . . "*scarce on our Reservation.*"

THE TILTED CITY

THE TILTED CITY

ROME sits, they tell me, on seven hills; and so, though I never counted them, does San Francisco. The only difference is that San Francisco seems as if she might slip off at any moment. A morning train decanted me into the city. But before I was half-way to my hotel, I was gasping at those vertical hillsides which had even scared the impassive Baedeker into comparing the local traffic to flies on a window-pane. My taxi mounted to the assault like a storming-party; its vitals roared; its nose explored the sky. I watched my feet mount slowly level with my eye. Alongside of me the cable-cars pursued their vertical career running, as Mr. Rudyard Kipling saw them, "up and down a slit in the ground." It must be very nearly forty years since that observant youth, just off the Yokohama boat, watched them "slide equably on their appointed courses from one end to the other of a six-mile street." The young man's eye was sharp enough; so was his tongue. But there is one point on which I can supplement his observation. He saw the San Francisco street-cars that "turn corners almost at right angles, cross other lines, and"—with a slight touch of hesitation—"for aught I know may run up the sides of houses." They do. If they did not, they would never get there.

For San Francisco is one glorious defiance of the laws of gravity. Streets, that should run level with the earth's surface, climb without warning into heaven or fall away with equal suddenness into the waters under the earth, leaving pedestrians to gasp on the edge of a sheer drop; I estimate that a cent dropped on the crest of California Street would gather speed enough to kill a horse in Market Street, unless it hit a Chinaman on Grant Avenue; and some feral magic had glued to the very summit of the city a vertical hotel, whose windows offer to incredulous eyes a stupendous mirage of house-tops ending in the blue Bay, the little islands in the Bay, and the green hills beyond. But I was always half afraid that San Francisco would slip off her hills into the water. If she did, I should certainly run to pick her up; and I feel quite sure that she would lie charmingly in one's arms for just an instant before saying "Thank you." It will be gathered that, where Mr. Kipling fell to a "big Kentucky blonde" and seven maidens more (including one Greek profile raised on beer), I fell in love with San Francisco.

The avowal seems impulsive. But what European could resist the sense, after many days and nights, of being back in the world again? To be in Keokuk, where the trains run to Peoria or to Dubuque, is to be in a dream; Bloomington is scarcely more convincing; and what could well be more insubstantial than Little Rock? But from here the steamers go to Singapore and Honolulu and Yokohama and Shanghai, into reality once more. The Old World stretches out an arm to claim its wandering child. Not that San Francisco is in any discreditable sense Old-World. For its tradition is quite magnificently of its own continent, with a fine profusion of Vigilantes, Forty-niners, and the corner of Washington and Montgomery where Casey murdered King of the *Evening Bulletin*, and the gallows on Sacramento Street, where they hanged the murderer to an audience of "3,000 stand of muskets and two field-pieces." Yet something older hangs in the air. You cannot call a barracks the Presidio with impunity; and if you carefully preserve the adobe walls of a Mission of Our Lady of the Weeping Willows, it will have spiritual consequences, even though you get there by the 16th Street cars and find it on the corner of Dolores.

So San Francisco is not quite the young embodiment of Western womanhood, before whose shrine (not forgetting the big Kentucky blonde and the Greek profile) young Mr. Kipling delighted to "roast a battered heart" in 1889. Not that she shows her years—was I unchivalrous enough to hint it? For she stands up, between Oakland and the Golden Gate, as young as the latest city summoned by oil out of the soil of Texas—and far better educated. But her eyes (I am going the way of Mr. Kipling again) are deep with memories. Remembered things haunt San Francisco—Drake and his Bible, the Mexicans, the Russian traders, the old sinfulness, and the gay bravery of 1906 when William James drifted volubly through the settling dust, clasping a box of Zu-zu gingersnaps and making psychological observations among the earthquake-stricken crowds. But where do memories haunt her more persistently than on a long street slashed round the steep escarpment of a hill, where the hanging lanterns have a new shape? Or is it the oldest shape of all? For there, behind the yellow faces in the little shops and on the corners of the sidewalks, what memories come crowding—memories of alleys in Canton, of queer sails reflected in the Yangtze, of still Buddhas in the distant sunshine, of the glow of painted silk and the pallor of jade. Chinatown is only a memory, recalling China much as an air tapped painfully from a piano recalls the surge and swell of a great orchestra. But even the replica recalls the glory of the original; and Asia hangs on the air of Grant Avenue, where the little dragons grin and joss-sticks burn and provision-merchants stock the most unlikely delicacies. Not being Mr. Kipling, one was not privileged to witness a midnight assassination through the smoke of opium. I got, indeed, no nearer than a little crowd that stood respectfully with a policeman round an upturned pair of boots; these noted, I withdrew. But all the air was heavy with the Old World calling; and as it called, I turned to it again. For we had crossed America and come out on the other side.

THE FILM RUNS BACKWARDS

THE FILM RUNS BACKWARDS
(*Transcontinental*)

ONE sunny afternoon it started. For the first time in months we were going East; and with the thought we were a little solemn. As the big car slid forward, all the faces in the porch faded into the shade behind them and California became a memory. Not quite a memory, though; for there was still the ride to San Francisco, to say nothing of seven hundred miles or so of assorted Paradise and desert that lay between us and Arizona. All down the road, where Santa Clara waved plum-blossom at us in a still farewell, the Sunday crowds in every size and shape of automobile responded to unnumbered invitations to chicken dinners; taller than ever in the spring evening, the big redwoods at Palo Alto watched the dark river of their shadows; and the empty streets in their Sabbath mourning seemed just a little sorry to see us go. We took a sad farewell of the Pacific in her largest, bluest oysters and strolled, uneasy wanderers with a night train to catch, through Chinatown. But another East was calling. The rueful little walk concluded; and, alone with our luggage, we dropped down the hill towards the station.

The big ferry moved punctually across the Bay; and behind us the tall city lights, like open windows on the sky, all turned to watch us go. A line of Pullmans waited in the hushed darkness of the station; our invariable darkey, guardian of Cæsar and his fortunes, received his guests; and the long train pulled out for Europe. A night slipped by; and as we rumbled into daylight, the big hills along the San Joaquin glowed blue and yellow with wildflowers. But the desert claimed us; and in the desert, being rash, we changed. We changed, to be precise, at Barstow, Cal., where the eager pen of Mr. Kipling once wrote of "engineers . . . in their lonely round-houses," and Providence, with the easy largesse of a desert time-table, had given us three hours to wait. Three hours can be a longish time; and three hours in Barstow are, I conjecture, longer than most. I saw the lonely engineers, noted their round-houses and, wondering how many of God's creatures had ever been a walk in Barstow, went for one. There is a fearful pleasure to be snatched from leaving stations at unlikely places. A strange attraction draws me to the untrodden fields surrounding railway-junctions; pioneers and Polar explorers have, I believe, the same sensation. Had I not, alone of the human race, taken a country walk at Bobadilla? I once visited a public park in Warrington between trains. And once, on a Sunday afternoon that is still remembered by the station staff, I left the Midland Railway Company's premises at Trent. So Barstow was a challenge. A lonely road wound uninvitingly over an iron bridge; a shrunken river crept beside a singularly forbidding kopje; and a reddish vista indicated the desert, waiting to be conquered. But the desert won. Subdued, I crept towards the station and waited for the California Limited.

That dignitary thundered in, shut down her brakes, received me, and departed. The loving care of unseen powers provided an observation-car with all the magazines and headed notepaper, a barber's shop, a manicurist, and a highly decorated diner, in which we feasted while this sumptuous pantechnicon sailed gravely across the bleached horrors of the Mojave Desert under a ragged roof of storm-clouds. (Some delirium suggested that Mr. Fred Harvey, purveyor of all good things along the Santa Fé, must have a brother Mo, who does the deserts.) That night we saw the Hopis once again, selling their beads at Needles in the glare of station arc-lights, and said good-bye to California.

The big wheels ground slowly up the long Arizona grades; and morning found us drinking hot coffee in the snow along the rim of the Grand Canyon. All day we stared across that scarred immensity, whilst our obedient Pullman waited in a siding. But in the evening we drew out again for Europe. Arizona handed us to New Mexico, and we were lulled with the long procession. Somewhere along the line an inconspicuous station announced the Continental Divide, where all the rivers began to flow (with us) towards the Atlantic.

We saw the Navajos at Gallup; our train, with ready courtesy, ran past the Indian houses of Laguna; and we got out to stretch at Albuquerque. Another night followed another day; and in the morning somebody announced that fresh trout from Rocky Mountain streams had come on board. So, as we ran across the corner of Colorado, we ate those miracles of catering; and that night we slept in Kansas City.

When sense returned, it was a Friday morning—Good Friday in Kansas City. The sound is slightly austere; but the reality was almost gay. For Missouri seems to celebrate Passion Week with open shops and crowds in the streets. True, one or two of the window displays appeared to strike a slightly devotional note; and, unless hearing erred, the Salvation Army gathered beneath our window greeted its Maker with something not unlike a college yell. But it contrasted oddly with our Spanish Easter of a year before, with the full-throated anthems of Burgos and the long funeral march of hooded men that wound slowly through the fading light of a street in Saragossa, where the borne effigies swayed above the crowd. Somehow one had not thought before of European austerity in contrast with the *abandon* of the Middle West.

That night we took the road once more; and all America seemed to flow past again in reverse order. There was the Mississippi, once seen far to the north as a sheet of broad steel lying between brown wooded banks under a brooding winter sky, where it flowed through Minnesota, homeland of Swedes and Finns and Letts and all the children of the Baltic—a slightly Baltic territory itself, flecked with snow and lacking only the little steeples and the bright cobalt of the sea. We saw Chicago again; and as the clouds hung low along the tall lake-front, we said farewell to Illinois. Once more, as California Limited transferred us to Twentieth Century, we passed the multiple Main Streets of Indiana. Farewell, farewell, the Middle West. There was Toledo, where the trains run north to Detroit and see the glow on the night over the Ford factory, where once I saw it from a plunging taxi in the snow. Farewell to Michigan. There was Cleveland, too, with the wind off Lake Erie, and the patient levels of Chautauqua. All our travels seemed to rank themselves outside the Pullman window; every memory that we had gathered came down to the station to see us off. We felt a little like Mr. Pitt, when he rolled up the map of Europe because he would not want it any more. Buffalo passed in the night; and we woke in the Hudson Valley with a broad river sliding past and houses that clustered, grew together, and became New York.

One more departure waited, as a taxi stole downtown through the evening traffic to the dock. A roaring concourse; lights and porters; then a gangplank; flowers in a waiting state-room; the familiar spaces of the ship; a last word to brisk reporters in the big brown room that waited for to-morrow's dancers; and the roar of ocean whistles. And so farewell, America. The piled and lighted city stood in the night outside. It veered a little, as we moved, and slowly slipped away. Then the lights receded; and we were left to the dark Bay, the Narrows, and the open sea.